1985

Marketing
Ambulatory Care Services

The *Health Marketing Quarterly* series, William J. Winston, Editor:

- *Marketing the Group Practice: Practical Methods for the Health Care Practitioner*
- *Marketing for Mental Health Services*
- *Marketing Long-Term and Senior Care Services*
- *Innovations in Hospital Marketing*
- *Marketing Ambulatory Care Services*
- *Marketing Strategies for Human and Social Service Agencies*

ABOUT THE EDITOR

William J. Winston is Dean of the School of Health Services Management, Golden Gate University, San Francisco and Managing Associate of the Professional Services Marketing Group, a health marketing consulting firm in San Francisco.

Marketing Ambulatory Care Services

William J. Winston
Editor

The Haworth Press
New York

Marketing Ambulatory Care Services has also been published as *Health Marketing Quarterly*, Volume 2, Numbers 2/3, Winter 1984/Spring 1985.

The Haworth Press, Inc., 28 East 22 Street, New York, NY 10010

Library of Congress Cataloging in Publication Data
Main entry under title:

Marketing ambulatory care services.

"Has also been published as Health marketing quarterly, volume 2, numbers 2/3, winter 1984/spring 1985"—
Includes bibliographies.
1. Ambulatory medical care—Marketing—Addresses, essays, lectures. 2. Insurance, Health—Addresses, essays, lectures. 3. Ambulatory medical care—United States—Addresses, essays, lectures. 4. Insurance, Health—United States—Addresses, essays, lectures.
I. Winston, William J.
RA411.M37 1985   362.1'2   84-27902
ISBN 0-86656-387-3
ISBN 0-86656-448-9 (pbk.)

Marketing Ambulatory Care Services

Health Marketing Quarterly
Volume 2, Numbers 2/3

CONTENTS

Preface

This issue is applied to Marketing Ambulatory Care Services. It follows the *Innovations in Hospital Marketing* issue which initiated the second year of the *Health Marketing Quarterly*. The number and variety of quality articles being submitted to *HMQ* by practitioners and academics continue to increase. I am pleased that the feedback about our prior issues applied to Group Practices, Mental Health, Long-term Care, and Hospitals has been excellent. It is hoped that the journal can continue being a major marketing resource for health practitioners. The next issue will be applied to Human and Social Service Agencies.

INTRODUCTION TO THE AMBULATORY CARE MARKETING ISSUE

This issue of the journal is one of the most exciting because of the tremendous expansion of ambulatory care during the last decade. Marketers and administrators are taking advantage of opportunities to experiment with the development of many new ambulatory services. Of course, the economic environment of the health care has dictated a need to develop services which provide alternative revenue sources, are more cost-effective and meet the new needs of the health consumer.

The text is broken into four major sections:

I. ORIENTATION TO CHANGING TRENDS TOWARDS AMBULATORY MARKETS AND STRATEGIES;
II. STRATEGIES FOR SPECIFIC EXAMPLES OF ADDITIONAL AMBULATORY CARE SERVICES;
III. EMPHASIS ON PRE-PAID HEALTH PLANS: HMOs, PPOs, AND INSURANCE; and
IV. FOUNDATION OF AMBULATORY CARE MARKETING: MEASURING AND UNDERSTANDING CONSUMER BEHAVIOR AND SATISFACTION.

xi

There is a significant change occurring in the health care industry. The product/service mix of the health organization is being altered to reflect the awareness of potential market opportunities, risks to avoid, new services to be developed, and new ways to deliver services. Many health organizations are mastering the ability to manage change, motivate entrepreneurial spirit, and improve the productivity of their services. This ability to manage change and channel creativity is dependent upon the organizationals internal capabilities, external factors, corporate culture, management styles and level of willingness and readiness to change. One way in which health organizations have begun to capitalize on market opportunities is to develop ambulatory care services. This issue's editorial discusses these abilities to manage change; to motivate entrepreneurial activities in health care; and to support creative strategy development and provides some common market strategies for urgent care centers, emergicenters, and same-day surgery centers.

SECTION ONE: ORIENTATION TO CHANGING TRENDS TOWARDS AMBULATORY MARKETS AND STRATEGIES

Section One of the journal lays the framework for the journal with excellent two-part articles by Dr. Alan Rosenstein. Dr. Rosenstein discusses in the first article the changing trends in the medical marketplace and how it is necessitating significant changes in the way traditional providers will practice medicine. He continues with the need to approach these changes with intensive marketing analysis and proper strategy development. A systematic methodology to strategy development for ambulatory services in the elderly market is emphasized.

This strategic approach to ambulatory services is continued in the second article with an application to hospital outpatient services. Dr. Rosenstein discusses the need to position the outpatient service and penetrate select marketplaces. He investigates the merits of market analysis, methods of opportunity identification and strategy selection as they apply to the overall outpatient environment in ambulatory care. This sets the stage for Section Two which demonstrates additional strategy examples for various types of ambulatory services.

SECTION TWO: SPECIFIC EXAMPLES OF STRATEGIES FOR ADDITIONAL AMBULATORY CARE SERVICES

This section begins with an excellent application of using the marketing mix as a framework for developing marketing strategies for emergency services. Avram Kaplan provides some key strategies which he has utilized in managing emergency services as related to the four Ps: Product, Price, Place, and Promotion of the emergency service.

The second article by Lynette Loomis switches to the marketing aspects of ambulatory geriatric care programs. Ms. Loomis discusses a specific case study of a successful geriatric service, Day-Break in Rochester, New York, which began to face financial pressures and formulated a marketing plan to assist in turning the center around. The plan concentrated on the identification of and strategy development for six major market segments for the ambulatory geriatric service.

The third article in Section Two by Dr. Sheryl H. Boyd examines the expanding new marketplace for fitness and health promotion aspects of ambulatory care. The paper presents the findings of a two-part survey conducted in Dallas, Texas that addresses the corporate viewpoint towards health promotion and local fitness programs. This area has become very important to organizations as they target their ambulatory services to the private business sector with greater frequency.

The concluding article of Section One by Dr. Dennis McDermott analyzes the evolution from a seller's market to a buyer's market as applied to an occupational health program. Dr. McDermott examines the redefinition of marketing missions, segments, and targets due to the changing market environment. This redefinition and segmentation are described by a marketing research study completed for an occupational health program.

SECTION THREE: EMPHASIS ON PREPAID HEALTH PLANS—HMOs, PPOs, AND HEALTH INSURANCE

The resurgence of health maintenance organizations; emergence of preferred provider organizations; and sudden interest in formal contracting has created an awakening of marketing ambulatory services via these new organizational structures.

The first article in Section Three explores the marketing of an HMO by Dr. David Schmeling and Dr. Winifred Schmeling. A controlled case study using a field experiment design is presented. The HMO studied was the Capital Health Plan in Tallahassee, Florida. One of the fundamental aspects of marketing ambulatory services is the collection of demographic and psychographic information for targeting the HMO. The case study used a questionnaire as the key marketing tool for the gathering of this kind of data and enhancing community awareness of the HMO.

The second article by Robert Sweeney and James Rakowski surveys an important part of marketing—the logistic characteristics of the prepaid sector of the industry. Their emphasis evolves into two crucial management areas: the nature of the cost-service tradeoff and the mechanisms for measuring, controlling and forecasting cost-service levels.

Dr. Robert Goldman shares his experiences with the marketing of one of the newest forms of ambulatory care—the preferred provider organization. Dr. Goldman offers some basic strategies for marketing a PPO as he has practiced in Maricopa County.

The final article of Section Three by Dr. Weldon Smith and Dr. Vinay Kothari examines the experiences of Stephen F. Austin State University related to its health insurance coverage. This article looks at the opposite side of the coin by systematically presenting several weaknesses that insurance companies have in common for implementing marketing strategies. Many prepaid ambulatory type services can learn from these experiences in order to develop more cost-effective marketing strategies and tactics.

SECTION FOUR: FOUNDATION OF AMBULATORY CARE MARKETING—MEASURING AND UNDERSTANDING CONSUMER BEHAVIOR AND SATISFACTION

This last section of the issue investigates the most important component of marketing—satisfying the health needs of the consumer. By thoroughly understanding consumer behavior the most effective services can be planned for and targeted.

Dr. Robin Scott MacStravic leads us into this important section with the discussion of the role of consumer satisfaction in marketing health services; the need to understand consumer and provider expectations from the services; the key criteria from which the consumer decides upon a provider.

The second article in this last section by Dr. David Andrus and Dr. Frank Kohout demonstrates the effect of consumer satisfaction with a local family practice on outshopping aspects of ambulatory medical services. Specific marketing strategies are offered for attracting the medical outshopper who is becoming a vital consumer group for ambulatory care services.

In order to work towards satisfying consumer needs in ambulatory care it is necessary to survey the organization's publics. Dr. Matt Elbeik outlines specific steps for the development and implementation of a patient satisfaction survey. The end result is not presented as an ideal format but allows for a flexible and integrated program as part of the overall health organization's management information system.

Relating to the ambulatory publics as effectively as possible has been emphasized in marketing for centuries. One of the most frequently used techniques for surveying consumer attitudes and perceptions in other industries is the use of focus groups. However, health care is only beginning to utilize this effective marketing tool. Dr. Troy Festervand introduces the focus group research; reviews the technique from conceptual and methodological perspectives; sets forth a suggested framework for the conduct of such research; and provides an illustrative example of its use in the health care field in the last article of Section Four.

Whether or not the reader is employed in ambulatory care, all of these fine articles by distinguished practitioners and academics provide excellent generic applications to marketing your services.

William J. Winston
Editor

Marketing
Ambulatory Care Services

FROM THE EDITOR'S DESK

Entrepreneurial Support for Developing Marketing Strategies: Example of Urgent Care, Same-Day Surgery and Emergicenters

CHANGING ENVIRONMENT CREATES OPPORTUNITIES

There is no doubt that the health and human service industry is facing some of its more severe economic challenges. However, amidst this economic turmoil, a surge of entrepreneurial activity has materialized to meet some of these challenges. New approaches to the health marketplace are challenging tradition in health care. It is unfortunate that we tend to dwell on the negatives rather than taking each situation and turning it into a marketing opportunity! Many health professionals have taken advantage of these opportunities and developed different types of entrepreneurial programs and services. For example, new health care institutions such as centers for psychiatric diagnosis, free standing maternity 'motels', wellness programs, home care geriatric services, preferred provider organizations, urgent care centers, ambulatory surgical centers, emergicenters,

1

stress management programs, and others have been stimulated by the current economic development. A considerable amount of this development has been due to the industry's ability to manage and channel entrepreneurship and creativity. This is also reflective of a changing corporate culture and value programming towards supporting and nurturing creativity and entrepreneurial activity within health care organizations.

One key example of changing values is the acceptance of non-profit organizations in developing money-making goods and services. Non-profit organizations have become much more imaginative and aggressive in their marketing techniques. Since the beginning of the 1980s it has become much easier to convince non-profit organizations that it is alright to make money and develop for-profit services. For example, the American Red Cross is marketing a first-aid kit; Planned Parenthood is selling private-label condoms and is considering a home for runaways; and a non-profit home care program is considering marketing self-testing diagnostic equipment. As government funding becomes much more competitive during the next few years, this entrepreneurial activity will continue to expand.

NEED FOR ORGANIZATIONAL SUPPORT FOR MARKETING CREATIVITY

Creativity is something which cannot be taught. There is an instinctive characteristic of 'being creative'. A major problem, for example, has materialized in our high schools and universities toward the outcomes of the archaic learning process. Unfortunately, creativity can be enhanced and supported but the educational systems still present the cycle of 'memorize, regurgitate and memorize'. Applying concepts and stimulating curiosity is a very rare educational experience for most students. Therefore, it is very difficult to develop creative skills and thought processes as a marketing professional. Marketing can be one of the most creative scopes of management if it is enhanced by a supportive environment. It is also one of the major stress aspects of being a marketing director in today's health environment. Health organizations are under tremendous pressure to develop new money-making services which can substitute for losses in reimbursed services. This pressure is being placed on directors of planning, directors of marketing, and administrators.

Many marketing directors are not trained, experienced, or personality-oriented towards being creative. Most marketing aspects of new service or strategy development follows some very traditional methodologies. The additional pressure is brought about by hospitals, for example, who have rushed to hire marketing directors because they feel they can be saviors. Usually, when marketing directors begin to come up with ideas for strategy development the medical staff, board or administration demonstrates they do not really understand the usefulness of marketing nor 'really' want to support the marketing function. In other words, they want results without taking the risk! The end result has been considerable confusion and a high rate of failure in marketing strategy development. In fact, the turnover rate for hospital marketing directors has been very high. One of the contributing factors to this transitionary trend is this lack of support or institutional consistency and direction. It is indicative of unaware administrators, board members and even directors of marketing. Marketing is not a short-term endeavor. Just as creativity and entrepreneurship, it has to be nurtured over time. In the area of creativity, even a small increase in efficiency, cost-effectiveness of a marketing strategy, and a small input of new insights can disproportionately expand the output of new marketing ideas that can yield rich dividends. Basic to creativity development is motivation. Most of the successful creative marketing strategies were formed from a strong motivational and optimistic base. This base can be created by the health organization with understanding and support for the broad scope of marketing.

The base of strong strategy development is related to taking advantage of marketing opportunities when they materialize or creating your own opportunities. One of the worst problems I have experienced with health planners and marketers is their negative outlook about their environment. If this attitude persists then the organization has lost more than half of the 'competitive battle' before it even begins. It is important to look back on history and be witness to the numerous similar environmental changes that have occurred in the health industry. For example, panic by medical providers, insurance companies, and hospitals over the 'PPO Movement' is spreading throughout the country. This panic is similar to twenty-five health policy changes enacted during the last forty years to contain health costs. The PPO movement brings opportunity as well as new risks. It is important to not panic and 'act before thinking'. I have observed, for example, some medical providers who have signed with over a dozen different PPOs in a geographic area. The interesting point is that that these providers have demonstrated a tremendous misunderstanding about what PPOs are all about even after signing with so many of them. In fact, many of the contracts were never even read by the medical providers! Getting on the bandwagon just because it is in fashion may bring dire results over the long-run.

COMMONALITIES OF MARKETING URGENT CARE, SAME-DAY SURGERY AND EMERGICENTERS

One of the fastest expanding ambulatory care opportunities has been the creation of urgent care centers, same-day surgery centers, and emergicenters. It has also become one of the most creative areas of hospital, group practice, and ambulatory care management. There are many commonalities between these ambulatory services in terms of marketing opportunities and strategies. However, their service mix, location and ownership can vary considerably. For example, these centers can be hospital sponsored, hospital associated, hospital based, satellites, or freestanding.

One of the key commonalities are the target groups to which these ambulatory care centers market their services. For example, all centers market to: existing physician staffs, potential physician staffs, patients, medical societies, nonphysician staffs, trustees, local regulatory agencies, third-party payers, corporations and businesses, media, medical suppliers, civil service agencies, the general public, and other health and human service community organizations. All types of successful ambulatory care centers are dependent upon the support of these different target groups.

A second area of commonality is the characteristics of the services which make an impression in the minds of the consumers. These characteristics include: courtesy, scheduling, cost, information provided, staff and physician attitudes, convenience, ambience, follow-up, opportunity costs, safety, and access. All of these consumer encounter characteristics need to be addressed in marketing strategy development.

An interesting third area of commonality has been the exponential interest in contracting, or at least serving, large groups such as corporations, unions, trade associations, universities, or churches. For example, some unique characteristics of marketing to businesses do exist for urgent care, same-day surgery and emergicenters. Industrial and occupational medical services are becoming a major boost to urgent care centers. Therefore, marketing to industrial medicine clients is becoming important as companies have seen their health insurance premiums increase by 200-300%. Businesses are definitely observing urgent care centers as a possible way to reduce these costs. In addition, marketing to industry provides urgent care centers with access to large groups of patients, such as members of HMOs or PPOs. For example, several urgent care centers in Seattle have over 400 companies under informal contract and 16,000 employees under formal PPO contracts. A great strategy for this group is to land one of the largest companies, and then others will follow. Credibility by association can be a great strategy for these types of centers. Then if employees are satisfied, a multiplier impact can occur with their families and friends. In addition, it is important to not overlook the hundreds of small businesses which are present in most areas. It is also important for urgent care centers to not assume they know what businesses want in health services. Don't develop brochures before surveying your target markets! Businesses also want quick feedback on employees. For example, they want centers to call and provide a status report within the same day of the visit, and of course, they want their employees to return to work as soon as possible. In addition, having a hospital as a 24-hour backup to the urgent care center is an attraction versus the free-standing center. It is important to decide what the center should really offer; what it is capable of offering; what businesses want you to offer for their employees; and how well the center can meet this demand. Urgent care centers have only recently begun to just scratch the surface of this potentially very large segment of the marketplace.

Finally, there are some common marketing strategies and tactics which are used for urgent care and same-day service centers. The following sample thirty tactics is not finite but they may be helpful as a checklist for marketing your ambulatory care center:

1. Continually obtain new resident listings and mail brochures.
2. Send letters and brochures or in person discuss centers with apartment owners and realtors.
3. Talk with large hotel/motel managers about posting brochures or working out an arrangement for discounts for their guests.
4. Talk with employee benefits directors of local corporations about allowing some information to be directed to employees.

5. Set up booths at conventions or trade shows holding their meetings in your local area.
6. Call each patient 24 hours after service is provided.
7. Maintain files for sending out birthday and Christmas cards, etc. to patients or local businesses.
8. Contact department store managers about having posters or brochures about the clinic placed in high-traffic areas.
9. Contact local businesses about referral sources.
10. Provide free bus passes for public transportation for those potential clients who do not have cars.
11. Arrange for parking discounts in local parking lots.
12. Encourage repeat visits by offering discounts or 'family packages'.
13. Advertise in airline journals and with travel agencies.
14. Get the physicians and staff involved in local social clubs, gatherings or events.
15. Have some of the staff publish articles in health journals.
16. Arrange for physicians to make home visits to those patients who cannot make it to the center.
17. Contract with a transportation firm for greater access for incapacitated patients.
18. Concentrate on nursing homes and board and care facilities in the vicinity for elderly clients.
19. Hire staff who are bilingual in dominant local languages.
20. Develop a community board consisting of representation of local groups, businesses and the general population.
21. Develop strong relationships with local and state medical and health associations, lobbyist groups and consulting firms for referrals.
22. Develop a strong tie to United Way since they make a considerable number of referrals to clinics.
23. Possibly investigate the use of appropriate billboards for advertisement.
24. Advertise in cultural journals such as play, opera, and symphony programs.
25. Develop a board of directors' subcommittee in marketing.
26. Contact local Social Security officials for potential referrals.
27. Possibly offer major employers an initial free physical exam for their employees if contracting can be negotiated.
28. Explore preferred provider, HMO, IPA, etc. delivery modes for the center.

29. Develop good working relations with local Blue Cross and Blue Shield Associations.
30. Patient and public surveys should be initiated to monitor effectiveness and community lifestyle and values.

As you can tell a wide range of strategies can be developed for your ambulatory care center. For example, on marketing plans I have monitored for urgent care centers hundreds of different strategies and tactics can actually be formulated, if creativity and entrepreneurship is reinforced by the health organization.

William J. Winston
Editor

SECTION ONE: ORIENTATION TO CHANGING TRENDS TOWARDS AMBULATORY MARKETS AND STRATEGIES

Ambulatory care delivery modes have been in existence for centuries. We can date forms of clinics, home care and outpatient care throughout history. Since organized health facilities are really an innovation of modern societies, people taking care of themselves, having someone visit them, or receiving same-day care is definitely not new to our health systems. However, ambulatory care as a formal form of medical service is relatively new and is expanding rapidly. For many years through the 1950s, '60s, and early '70s, superficial attempts were made to develop outpatient services across the nation. Unfortunately, these efforts were mainly tokens for the traditional 'sickness care system' that is prevalent in the health system. This is true despite the research that has kept proving the greater cost-effectiveness of preventive care over curative care. A society that spends over 10% of its GNP for health care, yet allocates only a small proportion of this total to ambulatory or preventive care, is approaching health status from a short-term approach. It is also no wonder why the economic cost of health care has risen so quickly when we operate a rather cost-ineffective system.

Containing health care costs is receiving a renewed interest by policy makers after numerous failed cost-containment attempts through the years. This renewed interest has stimulated changes in the reimbursement systems towards: (1) making the health client act more like a 'typical consumer' through higher deductibles and co-payments, a greater variety of alternatives to choose from, and greater amounts of consumer information about medical care services; and (2) placing set reimbursed limits on the suppliers of medical care for select services rendered and some incentives for developing more cost-effective modes of delivery. These policies are attempting to install a more traditional economic marketplace in health care where demand and supply are not guaranteed or immune from market pressures. Derived from this trend has been a surge of interest in lower cost forms of health delivery. Ambulatory care has become the fulcrum of this new search and development.

The concept of ambulatory care is a very nebulous one. There really is no set definition of the area of delivery because it reflects such a wide scope of different types of services. For example, think of the variety of 'different' services that are involved when we include such examples as: outpatient departments, clinics, wellness programs, holistic health centers, many forms of health maintenance organizations, preferred provider organizations, group practices, hospital emergency rooms, home care programs, same-day surgery centers, urgent care centers, emergicenters, hospice programs, meals on wheels programs, industrial health clinics, stress management programs, sportcare programs, rehabilitation programs, phone-in assistance programs, and even fitness, smoking and diet centers. The basic dictionary definition for ambulatory is the client's ability to 'walk in on their own power and will'. The newer characteristics of the ambulatory definition are related to the services 'going to the client', 'being of a very short-term duration', and 'respecting the client's ability to manage many parts of their own well-being'.

There will be many new forms of ambulatory delivery during the next decade as cost-containment for the consumer and provider dictate the need for: (1) providers developing new revenue sources for their programs plus need to better understand the changing needs of their consumers, and (2) consumers better understanding how effective it can be to receive care on an ambulatory basis and take care of themselves through a wellness mode. Marketing plays an important role in: (1) planning for these new services; (2) analyzing the marketplace for opportunities; and (3) communicating to and understanding the needs and behavior of the health consumer.

This first section is comprised of an excellent two-part article by Dr. Alan H. Rosenstein which surveys the historical development of the need for ambulatory care services in health institutions and leads us into the creation of specific strategies for ambulatory care.

WJW

The Changing Trends of Medical Care and Its Impact on Traditional Providers: Adaptation and Survival via a Marketing Approach

Alan H. Rosenstein

INTRODUCTION

The medical care delivery system in the U.S. is in crisis. Sky-rocketing health care costs, dramatic advancements in medical technology, and the increasing supply of health care providers and facilities have had a profound effect on the one time "traditional" practice of medicine. Spurred on by significant changes in government legislation and the growing influence of "entrepreneurism" and "consumerism" in medical practice, health care providers are now finding themselves in the midst of an intensely competitive marketplace. Many of these changes have occurred in the area of ambulatory health care services. The purpose of this paper will be to describe some of the influencing factors behind the shifting emphasis of medical care, the impact of these changes on traditional health care providers, and the adaptations that these traditional providers will have to undergo in order to meet the needs of the changing competitive marketplace.

Alan H. Rosenstein, MD, is Director of Patient Care; Chairman of Utilization Review Committee; Chairman, Physician Recruitment and Relations Committee; member of the Hospital Planning Committee at Marshall Hale Memorial Hospital, San Francisco, CA.

Appreciation is extended to Bonnie Harbourne, Karen Lillie and Ralph Keeney for assistance with the manuscript.

11

CHANGING TRENDS IN MEDICAL CARE

In order to evaluate the intricate nature of the changing medical marketplace, it is important to understand some of the social, economic, political and technological forces responsible for influencing the change. Although there have been many subtle changes occurring over the last two decades, the last two years have witnessed some rather dramatic changes in the way we deliver medical care. Some of these factors will be discussed below.

Health Care Costs

The major factors responsible for the dramatic change in the health care industry has been the overall astronomical costs of health care services. When the government first became involved in the health care business in the early 1930's (Social Security Act of 1935 — Federal assistance for maternal and child welfare, see Appendix A) it had no idea of what it was getting itself into. Even after passing the Medicare-Medicaid legislation in 1965 (PL89-97), the government was only spending $42 billion for health care, 6.0% of the Gross National Product. By 1975 the government was spending $133 billion on health care (8.6% GNP). In 1982 these costs more than doubled when the government spent $322 billion on health care (10.2% GNP).[1] President Reagan's projected budgets for 1984 and 1985 show continued increasing allotments for health care expenditures.[2] As the major purchaser of health care services, the government is obviously quite concerned about the continued escalation of health care costs.

As the second major purchaser of health care insurance, big business and major industries are equally concerned about skyrocketing health care costs. In 1981 Ford Motor Company estimated that it spent over $110 million for health care benefits. Chrysler Motor Company estimated that it "built in" an extra $350 per car to cover health care benefits.[3]

With no end in sight for this progressive escalation, government and big business are beginning to take some dramatic steps to curb this trend. These steps will be discussed in the next section.

Government Regulations

In the early 1970's the government tried several different approaches in an attempt to offset the progressive rise in health care costs. In 1972 the government established the PSRO entity as a mechanism for controlling and monitoring reimbursement of "acute care" hospitalized patients (PL92-603). Through the HMO Act of 1973, the government attempted to encourage utilization of HMOs as a lower cost alternative for medical care by providing federal assistance and establishing the dual choice provision for eligible employees (PL93-222). In 1974 the government tried to limit hospital expenditures and expansion of medical facilities by establishing the Certificate of Need (CON) requirement regulated through the local HSA (PL93-641). After achieving limited success with these initial legislations, the government made its first attempt to directly limit reimbursements in the early 1980's. In 1982 the State of California initiated legislation that allowed the state to contract directly with hospitals to provide care for Medi-Cal patients at "competitive" rates (AB 799 CA). In the same year the state extended this legislation to allow employers to contract directly with health care providers in a "competitive bidding" process (AB 3480 CA). In 1983 the Federal government passed the TEFRA legislation which established the DRG system of prospective case reimbursement for hospitalized Medicare patients. The impact of these later legislations had an even more profound effect on the health care system than originally anticipated. Not only was there a direct effect on reducing reimbursements for hospitalized patients, but there was a dramatic indirect effect of "deregulation" by allowing competitive contract negotiations to be negotiated between insurance companies, employers and health care providers. The competitive marketplace was encouraged. The framework for "contract medicine", "discount medicine" and "PPOs" had been laid. These concepts will be discussed in a later section.

CHANGING PATTERNS OF MEDICAL CARE

Although the political issues just discussed have had a definite effect on the future of the health care delivery system, these effects are complemented by the influence of other social, economic and technological factors. Significant advancements in medical technology, the emergence of "consumerism" and changing patient attitudes, and the infiltration of "entrepreneurism" and big business into medicine have had profound effects on the health care industry. These concepts will be discussed below.

Changing Patterns in Utilization

There has been a gradual but steady change in the focus of medical care from inpatient to outpatient services. Despite the fact that the American population is getting older, hospital occupancy rates across the U.S. have stabilized at the 75% level ever since 1960. In California the hospital occupancy rate has actually dropped from a high of 75.2% in 1957 to 68.5% in 1982.[5] There are many reasons for this change in activity. First, significant technological advancements have allowed many diagnostic tests and therapeutic regimens to be safely conducted in an outpatient setting which once required anywhere from 2-7 days of hospitalization to perform. For instance, the introduction of the CAT scanner has enabled precise medical information to be available in one hour that used to take several days of hospital testing to obtain (i.e., evaluation for obstructive jaundice with GI series, hypertonic duodenography, pancreatic scans, liver biopsy, etc.). Second has been the impact of PSRO utilization monitors which have reduced the number of "social" admissions and reduced the length of stay of "non-acutely ill" patients. A third factor has been the general economic situation and unemployment rate where patients are less apt to come to the hospital for elective procedures or less severe illnesses. Another factor that should also be considered is the changing consumers' attitudes toward health care, i.e., "consumerism". Patients are becoming more and more interested in being educated about the nature of their disease, its treatment, and efforts necessary for disease prevention. They are becoming more conscious about health care costs, convenience, and accessibility, preferring the more expedient "come and go" type of ambulatory procedures to the cumbersome, time consuming inpatient hospital alternative treating the same condition. The final factor that should be considered is the increasing influence of "entrepreneurism" into the medical marketplace.[4] The growing interests of big business and "venture capitalists" coupled with the recent legislations allowing medical institutions to advertise (Appendix A) has caused the medical system to be inundated with facilities that aggressively market and promote their products with the intent of making a profit. Most of these entrepreneurial trends have been in the area of ambulatory medicine.

Not only have utilization trends been shifting towards outpatient services, but sources of revenue have been shifting in the same direction. Hospitals obtain 80-90% of their revenues from inpatient

services.[36] With the impact of reduced occupancy rates and reduced reimbursements, the sources for revenue are beginning to
change. Recent Blue Cross statistics from 1968-1978 show an
18.6% reduction of reimbursement for inpatient days and a 137.6%
increase in reimbursement for outpatient visits.[7] Similarly, many
insurance companies are offering greater reimbursement rates and
lower deductibles for treatments performed in the less costly ambulatory setting.[8] The ambulatory alternatives will be discussed in a
later section.

Excess Health Care Providers

Besides the shifting emphasis from inpatient to outpatient services, the medical industry is plagued by the two other major problems. One is excess capacity and duplication of medical services,
the other is the excess number of physicians and other health care
providers. The excess capacity is a lingering problem left over from
the influences of the Hill Burton Act extending into the early 1970's
(Appendix A). The excess number of health care professionals is an
ongoing problem frequently referred to as the "physician glut."

Even as late as the early 1970's the government perceived that
there was a shortage of health care providers in the U.S. In the 1971
Health Manpower Act it continued to provide grants and federal assistance to expand the scope of medical schools and increase the
number of health professional students. In 1965 there were 7,400
medical school graduates. That number more than doubled in 1983
when there were 15,700 U.S. medical graduates.[25] The government further contributed to the problem when immigration laws
were purposely relaxed to encourage the entrance of foreign medical
graduates into the U.S. Non-U.S. citizen foreign medical graduates
obtained 17-46% of medical state licensures from 1970-1980. There
will be a 43% increase in the number of physicians entering practice
in the next decade. It is predicted that there will be a 70,000 surplus
of physicians by 1990, 145,000 by the year 2000. In 1960 there
were 148 MDs/100,000 population. In 1978 there were 171 MDs/
100,000 population. In 1990 there will be 245 MDs/100,000 population.[3] Other non-MD health care providers have similarly increased in number. In 1978 there were 20,000 paramedical personnel, in 1990 this number will double to 40,000. With excess
providers, excess facilities and changing trends in utilization, one
can begin to appreciate the competitive turmoil going on in the medical marketplace.

COMPETITIVE DEVELOPMENTS IN
HEALTH CARE DELIVERY

Besides the impact of recent government legislation, the changing practice of medical care, and the increasing number of health
care facilities and providers, there is another component of the
health care system developing that further intensifies the competitive nature of the medical marketplace by "removing" patients from
the "traditional" system of medical care. These developments will
be discussed below.

HMOs

HMOs are prepaid health care plans which provide comprehensive inpatient and outpatient services to a select group of enrolled
patients. Prior to the HMO Act of 1973, there were 26 Health Maintenance Organizations (HMOs) in the U.S. with a total of 2.9 million subscribers. In 1983 there were 265 more HMOs with 10.8 million subscribers.[11] The greatest impact has been felt in California
where more than 25% of the California population is enrolled in an
HMO program, 75% belonging to the Kaiser system.[12] The HMO
alternative provides a significant threat to the traditional medical
care providers in that they are "capturing" patients into their own
isolated system. As part of the arrangement of the HMO benefit
package, enrollees will only be covered if they seek medical care
from specific HMO facilities and providers. The impact leads to a
reduced number of potential patients available for the other private
health care systems.

Non-Physician Providers

Competition for patients is not strictly limited to physicians.
Other alternative health care providers have also been making
strong efforts to capture some of the patients from the traditional
health care system. This trend is particularly evident in California
where Naturopaths, Homeopaths, Holistic practitioners and other
related health care entities have been attracting more and more patients into their medical system.[13,53]

Proprietary Chains

A third major factor influencing the migration of "out of system" patients has been the steady emergence and proliferation of proprietary hospitals and for profit medical ventures. By utilizing aggressive marketing techniques, solid management expertise, and strategic location, these investor owned facilities have succeeded in drawing away a significant number of patients and physicians from the less efficient hospital competition. Whereas the overall number of U.S. hospitals has decreased by 10% over the past seven years, investor owned hospitals have increased by 40%.[14] In 1982, 1,045 acute care hospitals (15% of national supply) were either owned or managed by for-profit entities. They treated six million patients and generated $11.2 billion, earning $520 million in profits.[15] It is predicted that by 1985, for profit entities will either own or manage 25% of the nation's community hospitals.[16] Proprietary chains have also been in the forefront of entrepreneurism becoming heavy investors in the low cost alternative ambulatory care centers. They represent a double edged sword in removing patients from the private system of medical care.

PPOs—Discount Medicine

Another recent development affecting patient provider relationships has been the steady emergence of contractual relationships for health care. In essence these patients too are "out of system" in that they are limited as to the number of providers and facilities they can choose from. These Preferred Provider Organizations (PPOs) are established as a "dating service" between employers interested in cutting costs contracting with providers who are interested in increasing volume. Medical care is usually provided at a 15-25% discount rate.[20-22] California is again the nation's leader in their area with over 160 established PPOs being introduced since the passage of the Medi-Cal contract legislations. The emphasis on contract medicine and PPOs has been described as the "most rapidly growing development amongst health care delivery systems."[12] In a recent California Hospital Association survey, more than 40% of hospitals surveyed had experience with contracting at discount rates.[23] It is estimated that more than 40% of future private practice will function through contractual delivery at discount rates.[24]

ALTERNATIVE AMBULATORY CARE SYSTEMS

As mentioned previously, most of the impact from the changing medical marketplace has favored the proliferation of ambulatory care services and the establishment of new ambulatory care centers. Initially accepted by the price and convenience conscious consumers, these ambulatory care centers are now being encouraged by insurance companies as appropriate lower cost alternatives to medical care. The two major developments in this area have been in the development of Freestanding Emergency Centers (FECs) and Freestanding Ambulatory Surgery Centers (FASCs).

Urgent Care Centers—Freestanding Emergency Centers

One of the major developments in the area of ambulatory care has been the establishment of the Urgent Care-Immediate Care type facilities. Referred to by some as "Doc-in-the-box" or "7-11" medicine, and possessing such clever brand names as "Urgicenter", "Emergicenter", or "Convenience Clinics", these centers have made quite an impact in the medical marketplace. For the purpose of this discussion, these centers will collectively be referred to as Freestanding Emergency Centers (FECs).[26-31] The original concept of a freestanding urgent care center was developed in Rhode Island in 1975. The intent was to provide convenient non-emergency medical services to community inhabitants. By 1980 there were 180 operating FECs in the U.S. and in 1982 there were 600 operating FECs in the U.S. Future projections predict 4500 units to be operating by 1990. The emphasis of medical treatment continues to be for minor non-emergency episodic medical care. Whether or not these clinics are capable of providing true emergency services or whether or not the word "emergency" should be used as part of the center's title is a controversial issue which is still not settled at this time.

Why have these clinics become so successful? Some skeptics may argue that they're just a passing fad of big business entrepreneurism, others claim that they're successful because they steal the "cream of the crop" patients from the emergency rooms and doctors' offices. My feelings are that the centers have become successful because they provide a medical service package tapered to the demands of the changing medical marketplace. By adhering to the four basic principles of marketing, price, product, place and promotion, these centers are able to occupy a significant vacant niche in the medical marketplace previously ignored by the other traditional health care providers. The essentials of this market approach will be discussed below.

First of all, clinics are price conscious. Whereas the average fee for a typical ER visit is $115, the average fee for a visit to an FEC is $42. The average FEC visit is 33% less than the equivalent ER visit for the same illness. Second, the clinics are convenience conscious. They make a point of being accessible, open for extended hours and on weekends, and provide immediate and courteous service. In this way the clinics "position" themselves against the "inconveniences" of the ER and private physicians' offices. Third, the clinics are place conscious. They make themselves very visible and are usually located in such strategic locations as shopping malls and other areas with heavy consumer traffic. They are also conscious about atmosphere, style and aesthetics, positioning themselves against the "brick and mortar" type environment of hospital based ERs and the sterile environment of the typical doctor's office. Fourth, and probably most important, is that they are very conscious about promotion. These centers are very aggressive about marketing their strengths and positive features and spend a lot of time and money developing their image as a lower cost convenient health care alternative. They have already made a significant impact in the medical marketplace. This will be discussed in the next section.

Surgicenters—Freestanding Ambulatory Surgery Centers

The second major development in the area of ambulatory care has been the establishment of outpatient surgery centers. Referred to as "MASH meets McDonald's", these centers have coined such brand names as "Surgicenters" and "Minor Surgery Clinics", and like the Freestanding Emergency Centers, have also made quite an impact in the medical marketplace. For purposes of this discussion these units will be categorized into two major groups, hospital based Same Day Surgery Units (SDSUs) or Freestanding Ambulatory Surgery Centers (FASCs).[32,34]

The first successful freestanding outpatient surgical unit was established in 1970 by Drs. Wallace Reed and John Ford in Phoenix, Arizona. In 1975 there were five units operating in the U.S. In 1980 there were 100 units operating in the U.S. seeing 200,000 surgical patients a year. Future projections predict 270 units and 900,000 patient visits by 1986. The scope of services provided by these centers include all surgical and specialty procedures that can be safely performed in an outpatient setting.

Why have these centers become so successful? Taking advantage of sophisticated technological advancements in surgery and anesthesia, these clinics have followed along the same path as the Freestanding Emergency Centers by developing a medical service package tapered to meet the changing demands of the medical marketplace. Like the FECs, the centers have followed the four basic marketing principles to develop their niche in the medical marketplace. The only difference here is that traditional providers are responding to the pressures of the changing marketplace by establishing hospital based or office based surgical units of their own. The essentials of the marketing approach are very similar to the approach used by Freestanding Emergency Centers.

First the FASCs are very price conscious. The average cost of the surgery performed in an ambulatory unit is anywhere from 15-75% less than the same procedure performed in an inpatient setting. Second, the FASCs are also convenience conscious. Scheduling, registration and other inconveniences are kept at a minimum. The clinics are also place conscious, appropriate atmosphere and architectural design are given a high priority, and the clinics are usually developed in a pleasant accessible location. Fourth, and again probably most important, is that the clinics are very aggressive in marketing their product. Not only do they market directly to the public and physicians, but the clinics also attempt to market their services directly to insurance companies and industry as a lower cost alternative to surgery. The latter is quite important as Blue Cross and other major insurance companies are reimbursing outpatient procedures at a higher percentage rate than for the same surgery performed in an inpatient setting. Their impact will be discovered in the following section.

The pie is gradually shrinking.[37] Although many of the environmental forces have produced only subtle effects to date and many of the new alternative delivery systems are still in their infancy, there are certain trends recognizable which reflect the impact of these forces on the health care system. See Figure 1.

The impact of the changing utilization rates, with decreased inpatient admissions and reimbursements, and increased outpatient visits, is particularly important in relation to its effect on the traditional hospital based package of medical care and ancillary services. In fact many hospitals unable to adapt to these changes have already

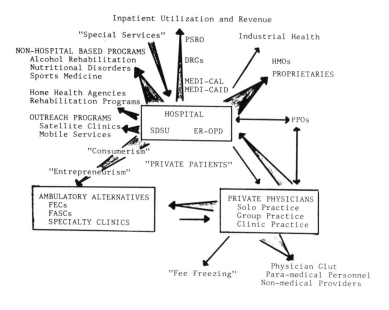

Figure 1: Environmental Forces and the Health Care System

Key: SDSU– Same Day Surgery Unit
FEC– Freestanding Emergency Center
FASC– Freestanding Ambulatory Surgery Center
PSRO– Professional Standards Review Organization
DRGs– Diagnostic Related Groups
HMOs– Health Maintenance Organizations
PPOs– Preferred Provider Organizations
ER-OPD– Emergency Room- Outpatient Services

closed their doors. Another 1000 hospital closures are predicted by 1990.[51]

HMOs continue to proliferate as a viable "low cost" medical system. The U.S. has 265 HMOs encompassing 4% of the nation's population.[50] That figure represents over nine million potential patients "extracted" from the traditional health care system. Quite an impact.

Proprietary hospitals also continue to proliferate. In 1982 there were 1,045 proprietary hospital systems in the U.S. treating more than six million patients.[15] Another six million patients extracted from the traditional health system.

The effects of the physician glut will be felt in 1990 when the supply of physicians will reach its zenith.[3] Not only is the patient pie getting smaller, but the number of slices is increasing.

The impact of the newer alternative ambulatory care facilities has yet to be determined. Many ERs have reduced their fees as much as 25-60% in an effort to compete with FECs.[27,28] The number of ER visits have also been reduced especially when FECs were developed close to their proximity. For the first time in 1981 national ER visits showed a decreasing trend, down 1.6% from the number of ER visits in 1980.[37] Similar effects have been felt by private practitioners. Many surveys have shown that physician office visits have been decreasing by 10-30% over the last several years.[52] Freestanding ambulatory centers probably have a lot to do with this trend.

Freestanding ambulatory surgery centers have had a somewhat different effect. Many hospitals and private physicians have been able to adapt to the changing emphasis on ambulatory surgery by developing same day surgery units and office surgery suites. With 20 million surgeries a year being performed in the U.S. and an estimate of 40% of all surgeries being performed on an outpatient basis, that still leaves eight million surgeries to be divided amongst these different alternatives.[5,32]

Traditional conservative health care providers can no longer sit back and expect patients to come to them just because they provide a health service product. Everyone is going to have to get out and aggressively fight for their part of the competitive medical market, and only the strongest will survive. Adaptation and survival techniques will be discussed in the concluding section.

ADAPTATION AND SURVIVAL

The traditional medical care delivery system can be viewed as a three way system, each part competing for the same group of private patients. The first part is the hospital base and its ambulatory extensions, the SDSU and ER-QPD clinics. The second part is the group of private practitioners in either solo, group or private clinic practice. The third part includes the newer ambulatory care alternatives including the FECs, FASCs, and other satellite specialty clinics. This system is graphically depicted in Figure 2.

The model in Figure 2 represents a dynamic system where each part of the triangle is exerting forces in an attempt to attract patients into their part of the system. At the present time it appears that the ambulatory alternatives are winning this battle. It is now time for the hospital based system and the private physicians to react in an attempt to recapture their share of the medical marketplace. This is

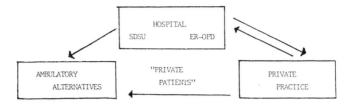

Figure 2: Traditional Health Care System

not an easy situation. The hospitals in particular are being placed in a very awkward position. On one hand they realize that they must expand their services into the outpatient market, but on the other hand they run the risk of antagonizing the private physicians who voluntarily use the hospital as their workplace. Some suggestions are presented below.

With the increasing pressures facing hospitals today, they can no longer rely on providing only acute care inpatient services. In an environment of reimbursement limitations, contract negotiations for discount fees, and declining inpatient utilization, the once immune hospital stronghold on medical care is now the major part of the medical system being placed in jeopardy by the changing needs of the medical marketplace. Hospitals must now undergo a dramatic change in focus which must include a total reassessment of their underlying mission, goals and objectives. Whereas hospitals used to concentrate on supplying costly intensive services to treat complicated acute illnesses, they must now concentrate on issues involving cost-containment, resource allocation and diversification into other medical and non-medical fields (see Table I).

Even the techniques and capabilities for survival are changing. During the years 1975-1980 more than 200 acute care hospitals closed their doors to inpatient medical services. At this time it was felt that it would be the small, independent, non-comprehensive hospitals that would fold. Indeed, several studies during this period indicated that the factors most responsible for hospital closure included bed capacity below 100 beds, non-comprehensive services, poor utilization rates, financial insecurity, and older inefficient facilities.[55,56] By analogy, it appeared that the larger multi-service medical centers with large teaching programs and the latest in sophisticated medical equipment and technology would emerge as the

TABLE I- HOSPITAL'S CHANGE OF FOCUS

Hospital Then	Hospital Now
focus on illness	focus on health, quality of life
concentration on major illnesses, emergencies	expansion to special services, minor illnesses
inpatient care	ambulatory care
secondary, tertiary care	primary care
staff relations - admissions, utilization	staff relationships - costs, LOS, discharge contract negotiations
quality of care - technology, services	cost effective care - profit margins
fee for service; reliance on 3rd party payors	reimbursement capping, contracts
service issues - products available conservatism	social issues - consumer needs entrepreneurism
portal of entry - E.R., PMD	portal of entry & exit - "capture distribution patterns"
one business	horizontal diversification "systems"
independent institution	vertical diversification - alliances, affiliations, mergers - "multi's"

survivors. But the tables have turned. With the changes in utilization and reimbursement, and the increasing emphasis toward ambulatory services, the larger institutions with their greater overhead and excess capacity, appear to be the institutions who are in jeopardy. Survival is no longer equated to size, technology or capacity, but more toward who can develop an appropriate niche in the medical marketplace and deliver their services most efficiently. The hospitals that emerge successfully will be the ones who have the capability and willingness to adapt to the changing needs of the environment. Successful adaptation is not just a matter of luck or intuition, but can only be accomplished through a thorough marketing campaign that includes comprehensive market analysis, strategic planning, readjustment of objectives and strategies, and appropriate program selection and promotion. Some of these approaches will be discussed in the following section.

MARKETING APPROACH

Market Analysis

The first phase of the marketing approach is the Marketing Audit. Each health care institution must undergo a thorough internal and external analysis in order to become aware of its place and potential in the medical marketplace. Internal analysis is a matter of self-examination of the services and characteristics that make up the integral working parts of the organization. External analysis is more of an environmental-situational analysis describing the nature of the competition and the environmental influences. Together, this analysis can be depicted as a "WOTS" analysis evaluating the Weaknesses, Opportunities, Threats and Strengths of the organization in relation to the marketplace. Each institution will have its own unique WOTS appraisal, and based on its own particular resources and capabilities, should be in a better position to react more appropriately to the changing environment.

Strategic Planning

The second part of the marketing approach is the process of Strategic Planning. By analyzing the information brought forth from the market audit and applying the process of situational analysis, each organization should be able to come up with a list of alternatives from which it must choose in an attempt to improve its position in the marketplace. The identification of possible alternatives and the selection of appropriate strategies best suited for each particular institution and its environment is a critical step in the marketing process. The goal should be to identify some yet unmet opportunity in the marketplace, and then try to fill this niche by developing appropriate programs based on the strengths of the institution and the weaknesses of the competition.

Strategy Selection

The third step in the marketing process is to develop specific strategies and tactics needed to achieve the proposed objectives. These strategies should outline the direction of where the institution is going, and how its going to get there. By utilizing the techniques of market segmentation, positioning, and promotion, strategies should be designed to penetrate specific target markets with a high degree of success. The selection of specific strategies will be discussed in the following section.

SELECTION OF SPECIFIC STRATEGIES

When confronted with the dramatic changes in the health care environment, particularly with the emergence of the new ambulatory alternatives and the increasing emphasis on outpatient care, health care providers can no longer afford to sit back and watch, but must react to the situation. They have three basic choices. They can continue to ignore it, combine with it, or compete against it.

For the private practitioner, the decision is easy. Since the competition represents a direct threat to the mainstream of their medical practice, their only real choice is to compete with them. For the hospitals, the situation is somewhat different. Ambulatory care had always been considered a secondary service, provided mainly to support the more intensive inpatient services. But with the changes in the marketplace, choosing to ignore the situation will lead to a continued loss of the "cream of the crop" patients to the ambulatory alternatives with the associated loss of needed revenues and potential patient supply to fill the vacant inpatient beds. The combination approach on the other hand is becoming more and more popular among competing health care facilities in their attempts to remain competitive in the marketplace. Many hospitals and health care providers have formed alliances, affiliations or mergers, in an attempt to share costs, gain access to capital, or develop a more comprehensive service package. In 1983, 40% of hospitals belonged to some type of multi-hospital system. This system is expected to encompass 60% of hospitals by 1990 and 80% by 1995.[46,48] If combinations are the systems of the future, it would definitely benefit hospitals to combine with some of the lower cost alternative ambulatory care facilities to make their comprehensive service package more attractive. The third choice is the competition alternative. In my opinion diversification and expansion into new markets is a very practical decision. Those institutions which are able to develop new products to meet specific consumer's needs will be the ones in the best position to survive by successfully penetrating new markets, securing new sources of revenue, and developing access to new sources of patients to support their other services. The remainder of this paper will discuss strategies for diversification with particular concentration on penetrating the ambulatory market and the elderly segment of the population.

Diversification

As depicted earlier in Figure 1, hospitals are faced with a number of different opportunities where they can diversify their products and extend their services beyond the confines of the hospital walls. Along the lines of vertical diversification, hospitals can develop special inpatient services in an attempt to fill vacant acute care beds.

Other special services and programs may be developed which are not hospital based. Along the lines of horizontal diversification, many hospitals have already expanded their services into the real estate market, hotel and restaurant business, catering service, textile and laundry service, and many other businesses as offshoots of their traditional service lines.[57,58] Although all of these efforts deserve merit, the greatest potential lies in diversification and expansion into the ambulatory care market.

Ambulatory Care

Extension and expansion into the ambulatory market is probably the most important avenue of diversification for hospitals to pursue. As the need for new revenues and new patient markets increase, and the inpatient census and reimbursement patterns decrease, hospital venturing into the ambulatory market is of paramount importance.

Although expansion into the area of ambulatory care may run the risk of antagonizing private physicians who may resent the hospital's encroachment on their territory, the private physician must realize that they too must react to the situation where they are losing patients to some of the new ambulatory care alternatives. Private physicians should be encouraged to participate in these programs rather than being antagonized by them. The hospitals must reassure the physicians that they are more interested in providing services for the 20-30% of the population that does not have their own private physician. These patients will subsequently be referred to physicians on the hospital staff, and represent an excellent new source of patients for these doctors. Similarly, hospital sponsored ambulatory care programs can provide a beneficial service for the private physician by providing medical coverage for his patients during off-call hours. If the hospital system treats a patient belonging to one of the physicians on staff, he can be secure in knowing that his patient will be treated effectively and returned to his care for follow-up treatment.

One other advantage gained by expansion into the ambulatory market is having an advantageous bargaining position for contract negotiations. By developing these lower cost alternative care options, the hospital stands in a better position to secure contracts with cost conscious employers and insurance companies, as well as providing a lower cost incentive for utilization by price conscious consumers.

What is the best way for the hospital to proceed? I feel that there are three major areas of the ambulatory care market that deserve particular attention. First is the need to provide for non-emergency urgent care type services to complement the services already provided by the emergency room. The second is the need to develop and promote ambulatory surgery services. The third is to develop outreach programs to provide services to the less mobile segments of the community.

As mentioned previously in this paper, the urgent care facilities have made a dramatic impression on the ambulatory care market. If these centers have the potential for providing convenient service for the more than 85% of the non-emergency emergency room visits,[28] the hospitals should definitely get into the urgent care business. This can either be done by developing its own satellite urgent care center, or expanding the scope of its emergency room to provide for and promote treatment of non-emergency illnesses. The former has its disadvantage in requiring a $275,000-500,000 start up cost.[59] The latter may require a two tier price structure for emergency and non-emergency visits. The latter has a great potential.

The emergency room represents the major extension of the hospital as its "portal of entry" for the community to obtain medical services. Originally intended to treat only acutely ill patients, the emergency rooms frequently discouraged non-emergency patients from using the system. Patients became antagonized by the attitudes of emergency rooms and their location within the sterile confines of the hospital environment. This opened the doors for the freestanding ambulatory care centers. Capitalizing on the patients' limited choices for obtaining non-scheduled after-hour care, their dissatisfaction with typical emergency room services, and the need for convenient, accessible services for patients who do not have a private physician, the freestanding centers have developed quite a niche in the ambulatory market. Emergency rooms are realizing that they no longer can survive on treating only "true emergency" patients. They must change their image from an acute illness, high intensity facility to a sensitive, accommodating, consumer conscious facility graciously welcoming all types of minor non-emergency illnesses. Emergency rooms will have to develop the same type of "big business" marketing techniques so successfully employed by the ambulatory alternatives. They must pay attention to price, place, product, and promotion. Emergency rooms should develop strategies to provide for price competitive non-emergency services. The place should be convenient, attractive, and emphasize expedient services in a pleasant accommodating environment. The product is already there, but should be further emphasized in support of the patients' sense of the potential "emergency" nature of his illness. Promotion should include "positioning" emergency room strengths such as staffing by experienced qualified medical personnel on a 24 hour basis, availability of hospital resources and backup, the ready availability of expert consultation, and the overall impression of delivering high quality continuous care. A special effort must be made to change the image of the emergency room to welcome non-emergency patients. This should include the usual promotional efforts delivered to such target audiences as the community at large, special interest groups and community leaders, businesses and insurance companies, as well as promoting the attributes of these services to the medical staff. One further tactic might include changing the emergency room sign to read "Emergency Room and Urgent Care Center." Changing the brand name can often make a dramatic difference. The hospital should make every effort to exploit the emergency room's potential for providing medical services to the community.

The second major ambulatory care strategy is to establish an ambulatory surgery center. Like the urgent care center, this can either be done as a freestanding unit or as part of the hospital base. With the prediction that 40% of all surgeries will be performed in an ambulatory setting, and the changing reimbursement rates for outpatient vs. inpatient procedures, it is again of paramount importance that the hospitals provide this service in order to avoid losing this financially attractive package to the competition.

The third major ambulatory care strategy is to develop either satellite clinics or mobile medical services as extensions of the hospital into the community. These outreach services would increase the hospital's visibility and presence in the area, tap into new potential markets, and establish a link between the hospital and the community population. The mobile outreach programs, which may include either a fully equipped medical van or a smaller vehicle equipped to make community "house calls", is a more attractive idea in that it not only can provide transportation for patients in need of more comprehensive hospital based services, but can also serve the less mobile segments of the community where access to medical care can be a real problem. Access to medical care is a major problem of the less mobile elderly population, and special attention will be paid to this segment of the population in the next section.

Elderly Population

Frequently referred to as the "graying of America", the over 65 age group continues to be a growing segment of the nation's population. In 1981 this group made up 11.6% of the population. In the year 2000 it is predicted that 18% of the population will be age 65 or older. The over 65 age group requires four times the amount of medical services than the under age 65 population.[48,60] Besides being a large potential market for health care services, the elderly population represents an important market segment for several other reasons as well.

At the present time the traditional health care system has essentially ignored any attempts to provide for a coordinated systematic approach to handle all the special needs of the elderly once they leave the hospital system. On discharge or transfer from the hospital, the elderly patient is confronted with a totally uncoordinated arrangement of rehabilitation facilities, nursing homes, boarding homes, special senior citizen centers, and home health agencies who are individually ill equipped to handle all the chronic medical, social, financial and domestic needs of the elderly. If the hospitals and other health care providers would get involved in coordinating these needs as part of the hospital system, it would not only improve the general care of the elderly, but would benefit the providers as well. With the impact of DRGs, it will be in the hospital's best interest to get patients treated as efficiently and expediently as possible in order to generate a profit from the prospective payment reimbursement system. Hospitals must now assume financial liability for care of the elderly patient. In 1982, 300,000 extra non-acute elderly care days were counted in the state of Massachusetts due to failure to place elderly patients.[60] If the hospital could coordinate a system of improved outpatient care for the elderly, the lengths of stay would be reduced as well as reducing many of the inefficiencies involved with discharge planning and placement process. In the face of decreasing utilization of acute care beds, hospitals should think about converting some of these beds to either self-care units, skilled nursing beds, or rehabilitation beds. Hospitals should also consider getting involved with the growing $21 billion nursing care industry.

Alignment with independent home health agencies, senior citizen centers or other board and care facilities is another good strategy to pursue. The purpose is to provide a more coordinated, efficient system of total care for the elderly, which would benefit all parties involved. On the ambulatory care side, it has been estimated that 50% of the elderly population does not have a regular source of medical care.[61] It has also been estimated that more than one third of the elderly population has some condition that limits their mobility.[62] These concerns give further support for the development of mobile medical outreach programs to complement the proposed hospital system described above.

Private Physicians

Finally we must address the problems being faced by the private physicians. Faced with the AMA's recent requests for voluntary price freezes on physicians' fees and the potential threat of mandatory freezes on medicare fees,[63] the threats of an increasing supply of physicians, the threat of hospital expansion into the ambulatory care market, and the increasing popularity of the new ambulatory care alternatives, the private physicians are really in a bind. Recent surveys have shown that doctors too are beginning to reshuffle their marketing mix in an attempt to counteract the competition. One survey showed that private physicians increased their number of house calls by 8%, another 5% extended their office hours, and more than 40% of the physicians surveyed had adapted some new type of marketing techniques over the past year.[49] Other physicians have adapted by entering into some type of contractual relationships with either IPAs, PPOs, or in joint ventures with hospitals. Needless to say, survival in the medical marketplace will require a dramatic readjustment on the part of the private physicians to meet the changing competitive trends in the environment.

CONCLUSION

The potential impact of the new trends developing in the medical care delivery system will have significant effects on the way health care institutions and physicians provide traditional medical services. The dramatic changes in regulatory legislation, reimbursement incentives and technological advancements have pushed the once immune system into a competitive marketplace similar to the world of big business. The pride of high quality care and personalized community service will soon be replaced by the bare essentials of capitalism and profit margins. Hospitals, emergency rooms and physicians are being challenged, and ultimate survival is at stake. It appears that the wave of the future will include more and more in the way of diversified multi-divisional health care systems patterned after the industrialized world of big business. One of the last strongholds of sensitivity and idealism has been absorbed by the corporate world.

REFERENCES

1. *Hospital Fact Book*, 8th Ed. C.H.A., Sacramento, Ca. 1983, p. 3.
2. "Comparing the Budgets" S.F. Chron. 2/2/84 p. 18.
3. "The Increasing Supply of Physicians, The Changing Structure of Health Services System, and The Future Practice of Medicine" A. Tarlov MD, NEJM vol. 308 no. 20, 5/19/83 p. 1235-1244.
4. "Entrepreneurial Trends in Health Care Delivery" J. Trauner et al., FTC Report Institute for Health Policy Studies U.C.S.F. July, 1982.
5. *Hospital Fact Book*, 8th Ed. C.H.A. 1983 p. 37-38.
6. Ibid. p. 39.
7. "The Health Care Market: Can Hospitals Survive?" J. Goldsmith, Harvard Bus. Rev. vol. 58, Sept.-Oct./1980 p. 100-112.
8. "How to Deal With the Impact of Alternative Providers" D. Glazier, Hosp. Forum Sept.-Oct./1983 p. 57-59.
9. "Unhealthy Cost of Health Care" Newsweek special report 9/4/78 p. 2-9.
10. *Introduction to Health Services* S. Williams, P. Torrens 2nd Ed. John Wiley & Sons, N.Y. 1984.
11. "Health Policy in the 1980s: Competition or Regulation?" G. Alpert, PhD, NERA Division of Marsh & McLennan Co. Sept. 1983.
12. "New Remedies" The Internist Nov.-Dec./1983 p. 15-20.
13. "Squabble Over Unconventional Medical Care" C. Petit, S.F. Chron. 11/11/82 p. 45-46.
14. "How For-Profit Hospitals Are Going After Your Patients" J. Hanelar, Medical Economics 8/9/82, p.275-232.
15. "Investor Owned Hospitals: Rx for Success" D. Robinson, Readers Dig. April, 1983 p. 82-86.
16. "Outlook for Hospitals: Systems Are the Solution" J. Goldsmith, Harvard Bus. Rev. Vol. 59 Sept.-Oct./1981 p. 130-141.
17. "Changing Philosophies in Medical Care and the Rise of the Investor Owned Hospital" R. Cunningham Jr., NEJM vol. 37 no. 13, 9/23/82 p. 817-819.
18. "Investor Owned and Not-for-Profit Hospitals" R. Pattison et al., NEJM vol. 309 no. 6, 4/11/83 p. 347-353; 370-372.
19. "Problem: Health Care Cost Containment. Solution: Investor Owned Hospitals" J. Reikes, Ca. Hth. Rev. Aug.-Sept./1983 p. 17-18.
20. "Competition-Getting a Fix on PPOs" K. Kodner, Hosps. 11/16/82 p. 59-66.
21. "Competition in the Health Care Market Place" E. Melina et al., NEJM vol. 308 no. 13, 3/31/83 p. 788-792.

22. "Discount Medicine: Price Cutting Is in Vogue with Doctors, Hospitals" M. Waldholz, Wall St. Journal vol. CIX no. 101 11/22/83 p. 1.

23. "PPO Activity in California Hospitals" C. White et al., Ca. Hlth. Rev. Dec. 1983/Jan. 1984 p.40-42.

24. "Marketing the Private Practice" E. Roberts, Ca. Hlth. Rev. 12/83 p. 50.

25. "The Coming of Corporate Medicine" H. Hiatt, Harvard Bus. Rev. Jan.-Feb./1984 p.6-9.

26. "Fast Help from the Docs in the Box" J. Parker, San Mateo Times, Ca. Four Star Ed. 5/31/83.

27. "Freestanding Centers Vie for Hospital Patients" J. Bendix, Mod. Hlth. Care Jan. 1982, p. 1882.

28. Emergence—National Association of Freestanding Emergency Rooms publication. June-October 1983.

29. "Emergency Centers Rise in U.S." R. Heffler, LA Times 5/22/82 p. 29.

30. "Impact of Fec on Hospital ER Use" M. Ferber, Ann. Emer, Medicine 7/83 p. 429-433.

31. "Experts Examine Major Issues Facing Emergicenters" J. Koncel, Hosps. 5/16/81 p. 83-90.

32. "Ambulatory Surgery" D. Detman et al., Surg. Clin. N.A. vol. 62 no. 4 Aug. 1982 p. 685-704.

33. "Mash Meets McDonalds" A. Field, Forbes 7/19/82 p. 85

34. Informational Bulletin American Surgery Centers Corp. Lynn Singley Chairman Scottsdale, Arizona.

35. "Ambulatory Care—Can Hospitals Compete?" S. Williams, Hosp. and Hosp. Ad. Sept.-Oct./1983 p. 22-34.

36. "Trends and Initiatives in Hospital Ambulatory Care" L.A. Burns, Am. Jour. Hosp. Pharm. vol. 39 May/1982 p. 799-805.

37. "Slicing the Pie Thinner" E. Friedman, Hosps. 10/16/82 p. 62-74.

38. "New Opportunities for Out of Hospital Health Services" J. Moxley et al., NEJM vol. 310 no. 3 1/19/84, p. 193-197

39. "Diversification—Broadening Hospital Services: What Makes Sense?" J. Goldsmith, Hosps. 12/1/82, p. 68-73.

40. "The Ambulatory Response" D. Harris et al., Hosps. 5/16/83, p. 69-71.

41. "Competition Spurs Ambulatory Choice" R. Gilbert, Hosps. 5/16/83, p. 67-68.

42. "Planning for Ambulatory Care Delivery Systems: A Market Segment Approach" D. Klegon, D. Gregory, P. Kingstrom HCM Review vol. 7 Winter 1982 p. 35-45.

43. *Ambulatory Care Organization and Management* Ross, S. Williams et al., John Wiley & Sons, N.Y. 1984

44. "The New Medical Industrial Complex" A. Relman, NEJM vol. 303 no. 17 10/23/80, p. 963-970.

45. "The Medical Industrial Complex: Our National Defense" M. Bromberg, NEJM vol. 309 no. 21 11/24/83, p. 1314-1315.

46. "The Big Business of Medicine" S. Dentzer et al., Newsweek 10/31/83 p.62-74.

47. "Reflections on Change in Medical Practice. The Current Trend to Large Scale Medical Organizations" E. Saward et al., JAMA vol. 250 no. 20 11/25/83, p. 2820-2825.

48. "Prescription for Profits" Time 7/4/83 p. 42-47

49. "Blessings of a Doctor Surplus" B. Breining, Wall St. Jour. 11/29/83..

50. *Hospital Fact Book* 8th Ed. CHA 1983 p. 48

51. "Hospitals Face 1000 Closures by 1990" M. Mannisito, Hosps. 4/1/82 p.23-24.

52. "...And Other competition You'll Face in 1983" H. Eisenberg, Medical Economics 1/10/83 p. 239-248.

53. "Current Controversy on Alternative Medicine" J. Lester, NEJM vol. 309 no. 124 12/15/83, p. 1524-1527.

54. "Chrysler, Hit Hard by Costs, Studies Health Care System" D. Rosenbaum N.Y. Times 3/15/84 pg. 10.

55. "Wide Range of Causes Found for Hospital Closures" D. McNeil, R. Williams Hosps. 12/1/78 p. 76-81.

56. "Urban Voluntary Hospitals: Predictable Closure-Relocation Pattern" A. Sager Hosp. Prog. Oct. 1981 p. 46-53.

57. "Non-traditional Revenue—Diversification for Profit" S.G. Kernaghan Hosps. 12/1/82 p. 75-81.

58. "Strategies for a Crowded Marketplace" R.N. Clarke, L. Shyavitz HCM Review Summer 1983 p. 45-51.

59. "Developing an Urgent Care Center" Amherst Assoc. Inc. Seminar 2/27/84 S.F., Ca.

60. "Why Acute Care Hospitals Must Undertake Long-Term Care" E. Campion, A. Bang, M. May NEJM vol. 308 no. 2 1/13/83, p. 71-75.

61. "Variety of Programs Show How Hospitals Market to Survive and Compete" Hosps. 11/16/81 p. 121-128.

62. "Long Term Care" D. Speltz Hosps. 7/1/82 p. 56-60.

63. "Freezing Doctor's Fees" Newsweek 3/5/84 pg.71.

APPENDIX A—HEALTH CARE LEGISLATIONS

1929	Establishment of first Blue Cross Plan
1935	Social Security Act health provisions
	First Federal assistance program; maternal & child welfare assistance
1946	1970 Hill Burton Act (PL 79-725)—grants to encourage construction of hospitals and other medical facilities
1965	Medicare, Medicaid (PL 89-97)—care for elderly and indigent populations
1971	Health Manpower Act (HR 8629)—expanded Federal assistance to medical schools & health professional students.
1972	(PL 92-603)—P.S.R.O. established. Federal monitoring of patient care—reimbursement implications.
1973	EMSS Act (PL 93-154) development of comprehensive area-wide emergency medical service system.
1973	HMO Act (PL 93-222)—Assistance for development of HMO's. Dual choice provision.
1974	National Health Planning and Resources Act (PL 93-641) established HSA's—CON; capital expenditures limitations
1982	(SB 930 CA)—related CON requirements
1982	(AB 799 CA)—Allow state to contract with hospitals for Medi-Cal coverage. Also allowed private insurance companies to contract with health care providers in a competitive bidding process.
1982	(AB 3480 CA)—Allowed employers to contract with health care providers in a competitive bidding process. (P.P.O.'s)
1983	Tax Equity and Fiscal Responsibility Act—Established prospective payment per case reimbursement for inpatient care (DRG's)
1983	Blue Cross Prudent Buyer Option
1977	Supreme Court decision Bates v. State of Arizona (433 US 350) paved the beginnings of professional advertising
1977	AHA approval of advertising if "truthful and accurate" and "not done at the expense of the competitor"
1979	FTC v. AHA (50 USLW 4313)—FTC banning AHA from interfering with advertising attempts by its members

Ambulatory Medicine: Opportunity Analysis and Strategy Selection

Alan H. Rosenstein

INTRODUCTION

As discussed in detail in the last issue of *Health Marketing Quarterly*, the changing economic, social and regulatory environment has produced dramatic changes in the one time traditional health care delivery system.[1] At one end of the spectrum is the traditional hospital-based system of medical care. With the growing emphasis on outpatient care, progressively declining inpatient utilization rates, and the first in a series of inpatient reimbursement limitations already upon us, hospitals are being faced with some major challenges with ultimate survival at stake. At the other end of the spectrum is the traditional private practice office-based system of medical care. With the increasing success of the new freestanding "entrepreneurial" ambulatory care centers, the growing supply of physicians and other health care providers, and the potential threats of reimbursement limitations, the one time private practice sanctuary of outpatient medical care is being threatened as "everybody else" gets into the outpatient market. Private practitioners too are being faced with some major challenges; is ultimate survival at stake?

In an effort to counter some of these challenges, hospitals and private practitioners have embarked on some interesting adventures. Hospitals have attempted to diversify their services by not only expanding into medically related fields, but by also expanding into such non-traditional areas as real estate, laundry and textile services, food and catering services, and even direct entry into the res-

Alan H. Rosenstein, MD, is Director, Patient Care, Marshall Hale Memorial Hospital, San Francisco, CA.

taurant, motel and hotel business.[2-4] Private practitioners have responded by reviving the all but forgotten house call, extending their office hours to evenings and weekends, and adapting the once considered "immoral and unethical" marketing and advertising techniques so successfully employed by big business in an effort to rejuvenate their dwindling practices.[5,6]

The following discussion will focus on the changes in the ambulatory-outpatient health care delivery system and the challenges being faced by hospitals and private practitioners in this arena. Emphasis will be placed on recognizing alternative courses of action and selection of specific strategies in an effort to survive in the new environment.

BACKGROUND AND MARKET POTENTIAL

The growing emphasis on ambulatory care has spawned a new breed of ambulatory care alternatives that have already developed a significant niche in the medical marketplace. Although traditional health care providers have extended their reach into the outpatient market by developing satellite medical clinics and emergency rooms, and office-based medical centers and surgical mini-suites, most of the success has been enjoyed by the new Freestanding Urgent Care-Emergency Centers (FECs) and the Freestanding Ambulatory Surgical Centers (FASCs) that have been springing up all across the nation. In 1978 there were 80 FECs operating nationwide. By 1982 there were over 600 FECs in operation, and the number is projected to increase to 4,500 centers operating by the year 1990.[7,8] In 1970 the first FASC was established and by 1980 there were over 100 FASCs in operation treating over 200,000 patients a year. This number is projected to increase to 270 centers by 1986, treating over 900,000 patients a year.[9]

Why have these centers become so successful? In general, much of their success is based on their philosophical approach toward the delivery of medical services capitalizing on the current trends of "consumerism" and "entrepreneurism."[10,11] More specifically their success is based on their strong adherence to the four basic principles of marketing: product, place, price and promotion. By providing accessible, convenient services delivered in a pleasant environment at a competitive price, backed by an aggressive promotional and advertising campaign, these centers have made a significant impact on the outpatient market. Emergency room visits are down as much as 10% in some areas, and many emergency rooms have been forced to reduce their fees by as much as 25-60% in order to compete with nearby centers.[12-16] Office visits to private physicians have been estimated to be off by as much as 10-30% in some areas, partly related to the impact of these centers.[17] With the current trends favoring outpatient to inpatient surgeries, it is estimated that 40% of all surgeries will be conducted on a "come and go" ambulatory basis.[9,18]

What kind of impact does this have on the overall outpatient market? As illustrated in Table I, there were more than 248,000,000 outpatient visits in the United States in 1982, including 76,000,000 emergency room visits.[19] If the ambulatory care alternatives indeed have the potential for attracting more than 10% of this market, this means that more than 25,000,000 patients will be "extracted" from this traditional health care delivery system. Similarly, there were more than 500,000,000 office visits made to private practitioners in 1982.[20] If the ambulatory care alternatives also attract 10% of this market, more than 50,000,000 patients will be "extracted" from this traditional health care system. In 1982 there were over 20,000,000 surgeries performed in the United States.[21] If 40% of these surgeries can now be done on an outpatient basis, hospitals run the risk of "losing" more than 8,000,000 surgeries to the ambulatory centers.

Admittedly, these statistics may overexaggerate the actual numbers involved, but the point to be made is that these ambulatory

TABLE I- HOSPITAL OUTPATIENT VISITS AND SURGERY- 1972-1982

	Outpatient Visits	Emergency Visits*	Surgical Operations
1972	162,668,000	55,660,000	14,768,063
1973	173,068,000	61,306,000	15,412,808
1974	188,940,000	66,785,000	16,193,348
1975	190,672,000	68,937,000	16,663,846
1976	201,247,000	71,864,000	16,832,106
1977	198,708,000	72,607,000	17,144,447
1978	201,931,000	76,123,000	17,150,124
1979	198,778,000	76,328,000	18,268,581
1980	202,310,000	77,245,000	18,767,666
1981	202,768,000	77,493,000	19,236,206
1982	248,124,000	75,981,000	19,593,639

* Emergency visits are a component of outpatient visits.

SOURCE: Hospital Statistics, American Hospital Association, Chicago, Ill. , 1972-1983

care alternatives have a significant potential to capture a large part of the outpatient market. This potential must be kept in mind when deciding on alternative courses of action and strategy selection which will be discussed in the next two sections.

MARKET ANALYSIS AND STRATEGY SELECTION

As discussed in the previous sections, the need for expansion and development of the outpatient-ambulatory market is essential. Although on the surface it may appear as if the opportunities for outpatient diversification are abundant, selection of any particular opportunity is a crucial decision which must be made on an individual case by case basis. Appropriate opportunity selection can only be performed after conducting a comprehensive market analysis.

In a broad sense, Market Analysis can be defined as a series of procedures to gather information about the environment, relate this information to the specific needs of the individual health care provider concerned, and then develop an appropriate course of action matching the capabilities and limitations of the provider with the best opportunities available. The specific stages involved in conducting a comprehensive market analysis are variable. The following discussion will be based on the Market Analysis model described in Figure 1.

The Situation Analysis phase of the analysis model represents the information gathering stage. Internal Analysis includes the analysis

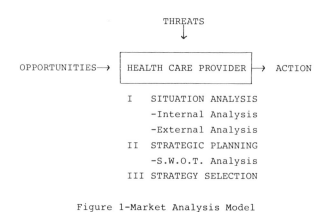

```
                        THREATS
                          ↓

OPPORTUNITIES→  │ HEALTH CARE PROVIDER ├→  ACTION

                I    SITUATION ANALYSIS
                     -Internal Analysis
                     -External Analysis
                II   STRATEGIC PLANNING
                     -S.W.O.T. Analysis
                III  STRATEGY SELECTION
```

Figure 1-Market Analysis Model

of all data related to the inherent qualities of the provider concerned. For physicians, this would include analysis of office space potential and limitations, analysis of services provided, analysis of physician practice patterns, and analysis of the patients served. For hospitals, internal analysis includes analysis of the physical plant, including potential capabilities and limitations, analysis of services provided, analysis of physician behavior and utilization patterns, and demographic analysis of the population served. External analysis includes the analysis of all data related to the external environment of the provider. For both physicians and hospitals, external analysis includes intensive evaluation of the competition, evaluation of present services available and future services planned, knowledge of the regulatory and reimbursement environment, and a constant awareness of the changing trends in the medical marketplace.

The second phase in the analysis model is the Strategic Planning stage. In this stage, all the information gathered from the analysis stage is transposed into a format that directly relates this information to the specific attributes of the provider. The usual format for this type of arrangement is referred to as a S.W.O.T. analysis. With this analysis, the information is categorized as being either a Strength, Weakness, Opportunity, or Threat as it relates to the particular situation of the provider concerned.

The third phase in the analysis model is the Strategy Selection stage. After weighing the merits of each category in the S.W.O.T. analysis each provider will be faced with a number of different possible opportunities for consideration. The selection of the most appropriate alternatives and strategies represents the most crucial aspect of the market analysis procedure and will be discussed in more detail.

Specific strategy selection is a difficult task and there is no standardized way to accomplish it. Approaches have varied from sheer intuition to comprehensive computerized multi-variant decision analysis. The practical approach is somewhere in between.

Whatever approach is adapted, the most important aspect to consider is that each opportunity be evaluated in a consistent manner, related to the specific attributes of the individual provider concerned. Although there are many different categories that may be applied, each provider should select only those categories which play an integral role for decision analysis. In general, opportunities should be evaluated in regard to their consistency with the provider's goals and objectives, they should have staff and community acceptance, and they should improve the provider's community image. More specifically, opportunities should be rated in regard to their potential market impact, their cost/reimbursement ratio, and the resources and time required for implementation. Once these opportunities have been evaluated in this manner, appropriate selection can be made. An example of such an evaluation and selection process is illustrated in Figure 2.

By evaluating each alternative in this way, opportunities are compared in a consistent manner in relation to the overall provider perspective, and in relation to each other. Add some qualitative "intuition" to the quantitative model, and we are now ready to proceed to the next section on specific strategies.

SPECIFIC STRATEGIES

At the present time ambulatory care-outpatient medicine is a growing wide open field that can be approached from two basic view points. The first approach is to develop new outpatient programs and services that cater to specific community needs. The second approach is to simply "rearrange" existing outpatient services into a new package of medical services created with more "public appeal." These concepts will be discussed in relation to the Categories of Outpatient Services presented in Table II.

		Consistent with Goals	Staff Support	Community Support	Image	Market Share	Cost/Reimbursement	Implementation	Other Criteria
I	Urgent Care	-	-	-	-	-	-	-	-
II	Sports Medicine	-	-	-	-	-	-	-	-
III	Mobile Services	-	-	-	-	-	-	-	-

Rating Scale: 5-positive   3-no impact   1-negative   TOTAL

Figure 2-Quantitative Selection Criteria

TABLE II- CATEGORIES OF OUTPATIENT SERVICES

```
I    Development of Special Programs
          -Behavior Modification Programs
          -Concentrated Specialty Programs
          -Special Service Programs
II   Development of Market Specific Programs
          -Elderly Care Market
          -Womens Clinics, Adolescent Centers
          -Industrial-Occupational Health Centers
III  Development of General Outpatient Care Programs
          -Urgent Care Centers
          -Same Day Surgery Units
IV   Other Outpatient  Adventures
          -Satellite Clinics and Emergency Rooms
          -Storefront Offices
          -Mobile Medical Services
V    Contract Negotiations
```

SPECIFIC OUTPATIENT PROGRAMS

The first category includes development of selective outpatient programs that meet specific community needs. Examples would include Behavior Modification Programs (eating disorders, nutrition, smoking, alcohol and drug rehabilitation centers), Concentrated Specialty Programs (sports medicine, cardiac rehabilitation) or Special Service Programs (education, wellness centers, diagnostic centers and the like). If we subject these programs to the evaluation and selection process discussed in the previous section, we will find these programs advantageous in filling a community need, but somewhat limited in their ability to service a large part of the outpatient market.

The second category represents another specific approach to the outpatient market by developing programs that cater to specific segments of the community. These programs include development of special outpatient programs for the elderly, development of special treatment centers for women and adolescents, or development of occupational health centers that cater to the needs of the industrial market. With the increased attention toward comprehensive outpatient services for the elderly, the increasing preference for specialized treatment in women's and adolescent centers, and growing industry concerns about the costs of health care and employee productivity, these programs offer a significant potential for securing a large part of the outpatient market.[1,28,29]

Although the first two categories represent excellent opportunities for development of concentrated outpatient programs, the remainder of this discussion will concentrate on program developments in the general ambulatory care market. In my opinion, it is the routine everyday medical and surgical needs of the community that constitute the "bread and butter" care of the outpatient market, and outpatient development along these lines will have the greatest market potential.

GENERAL OUTPATIENT PROGRAMS

The general ambulatory care-outpatient market includes treatment for all those ailments and medical complaints that cause patients to seek medical advice. With over 500,000,000 office visits, 200,000,000 outpatient visits and 8,000,000 ambulatory surgeries each year, this represents quite a substantial market. The situation is further intensified by the increasing number of practicing physicians, the increasing number of para-medical personnel, and the increasing numbers of non-physician providers practicing Chiropractory, Homeopathy, Naturopathy and Holistic Medicine.[30,31] Although each one of these providers have been able to secure a portion of the outpatient market, the biggest threat to the traditional providers has come from the dramatic success of the ambulatory care alternatives.

If the freestanding centers represent the most significant threat to the bread and butter of traditional medicine, how should Hospitals and private practitioners react to the situation? There are three basic options: ignore, combine or compete. Each one of these alternatives will be discussed in relation to the model depicted in Figure 3.

Outpatient Medical Care-Urgent Care Centers (FECs)

Cleverly titled "Convenience Clinics, Urgicenters or Emergicenters," but frequently referred to as "7-11" or "Doc-in-the-Box" medicine, the FECs clearly have the dynamics of patient flow headed in their direction. The FECs have become successful because they create an image of providing convenient, accessible, cost efficient ser-

I   General Medical Care

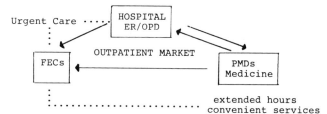

II   Ambulatory Surgical Care

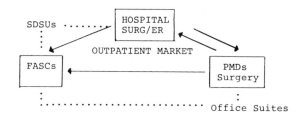

Figure 3- Dynamic Changes in the Outpatient Market

vices for non-scheduled medical care. By positioning themselves against the brick and mortar sterile image of the hospitals, the antagonisms of the inefficient intensive care conscious emergency rooms, and the inconveniences of long waiting periods and inaccessibility of private physicians, the FECs have become a major threat to traditional health care providers. Out of the three alternative possibilities, adopting the ignore alternative will do little to change the pattern of patient flow.

The competition alternative provides a much more realistic approach to the situation. The only way hospitals and private practitioners can compete with the FECs is to develop service packages based on the same successful formula utilized by these centers. This includes an awareness of the current trends of consumerism and entrepreneurism, and concentration on the four basic marketing principles discussed above. We will call this the "change the storefront window" approach.

In most cases, hospitals and physicians already provide all the basic medical services needed to supply the product, but need some assistance in repackaging the product to stimulate consumer appeal. For hospitals this means developing a convenient, attractive, cost effective package of medical services that "welcomes" the everyday non-scheduled minor complaints of the consumer. This can either be done by establishing its own urgent care center (freestanding or hospital based), or changing the characteristics of the basic emergency room service to welcome such illnesses. Establishing a separate freestanding urgent care center may not be the best approach, as estimated start up costs vary between $300,000-600,000.[32,33] Establishing an urgent care center as part of the hospital base is feasible in that it not only saves significant start up costs, but it can utilize existing hospital services. This can either be done as a separate service entity, or as part of the emergency room service.

As mentioned previously the product is not only there, but it should be promoted as having 24 hour staffing by well trained, well qualified personnel, having complete emergency capabilities, and having readily available hospital back up in case of the need for more intensive services or admission. In this way the hospital can "position" this service against some of the shortcomings of the freestanding centers. In regard to place, the only readjustment to be made is to simply change the attitudes of typical emergency rooms to welcome the minor complaints of the consumers and to treat these complaints in a convenient and expedient fashion. The major adjustment comes in the price category. A multi-tier price system will have to be established to separate minor urgent care cases from true emergency cases. This can either be done as a simple two tier price system separating urgent and emergency care, or on a multi-tier price system ranging from brief-limited-intermediate-emergency services. Adjustments will have to be made in regard to the facility fee, physician charges, and use of ancillary services, and should be based on a severity of illness-intensity of service criteria. Facility fees can be rated as to the amount of time and resources consumed. Physician fees can be adjusted by appropriate RVS coding. Ancillary service fees can either be adjusted across the board or have reduced prices for such common procedures as the chest x-ray, CBC, and U/A, with regular prices remaining for all other procedures. Categorization can be made by the interviewing nurse or treating physician in direct communication with the patient. The fourth major category is promotion. Now that the package has been redesigned, it must be re-introduced to the public under a different name that includes the concept of urgent care in the title. Now we've not only changed the storefront window, but we've changed the brand name as well, a very important concept needed to change the usual consumer impression about hospital based services when competing with the FECs. The entire concept must then be promoted to the community by the conventional advertising and marketing techniques.

Adjustment to the freestanding centers by private physicians is a more difficult task. The product is there, and the price is there, but the major readjustments must occur in the place and promotion categories. In regard to place, the physicians will have to become more accessible and more accommodating, and try to improve some of the inefficiencies of their office practice that contribute to patient inconveniences. Promotion should include enhancement of the usual physician-patient relationship and continuity of care, two of the basic shortcomings of the episodic care provided by the freestanding centers.

One further adjustment must be made by both hospitals and private physicians as they compete in the same arena. Hospitals beginning urgent care centers must be sure not to antagonize staff physicians by giving them the impression that they are entering into direct competition for the outpatient market. Hospitals must make it clear that they are only interested in attracting patients who are not already aligned with private physicians, and that if private patients are seen, they will be referred back to their private physicians for follow-up and continued care. With this basic intention in mind; private physicians should look forward to these centers as a potential source of new patient referrals, and as a convenient cost-effective place for their patients to be seen during non-office hours. It is mandatory that hospitals and private physicians work together in order to meet the challenges posed by these freestanding centers.

The final alternative is the combination alternative. Instead of developing their own centers, hospitals can make arrangements with already existing centers to provide transportation or support if there is a need for more intensive services or hospital admission. In this way hospitals will at least gain more access to the more acutely ill patients which can then be referred to private physicians on their staff for consultation and treatment.

Outpatient Surgical Care-Ambulatory Surgical Centers (FASCs)

Usually referred to as "Surgicenters" or "mobile M*A*S*H units," the FASCs have also made a significant impact on the outpatient surgical market. Like FECs, the FASCs have become successful because of their emphasis on the latest trends of consumerism and entrepreneurism, and the delivery of their product in conjunction with the basic principles of marketing.

When surgical and anesthesia techniques reached the point where patients were able to return home soon after surgery, a new era of "come and go surgery" was born. Capitalizing on these technological advancements, the FASCs began their assault on the outpatient surgical market. Accommodating the consumer's needs, the services are quick, efficient, less costly, delivered in a convenient, pleasant environment, and are specifically developed to allow the patient to return home on the same day of surgery. But even more important than accommodating the needs of the patient, the FASCs also cater directly to the surgeon as the referring physician. By providing an efficient, convenient, well-developed system, the surgeons appreciate less bureaucratic and administrative delays, and don't have to worry about their cases being delayed or "bumped" by another surgical case as frequently occurs in an inpatient hospital setting. Patients like it, surgeons like it, and the system is working well.

Similar to the situation with the FECs, the hospitals and private practitioners are faced with another dilemma of how to react to the situation. The circumstances are different but the options are the same: ignore, compete or combine.

Adapting the ignore alternative would mean running the risk of losing scheduled elective minor surgery patients and unscheduled minor surgery cases to the surgicenters. Given the potential of the outpatient surgical market, this is a risk that should not be taken.

Again, the competition alternative provides a much more practical solution to the problem. Hospitals have always had the capacity to perform minor surgeries, but they usually took a secondary place to the more intensive major surgeries. However, with 40% of the market devoted to ambulatory surgery, more and more hospitals are creating Same Day Surgery Units (SDSU) to meet this challenge. As many as 70% of all hospitals are estimated to have specific SDSUs devoted to ambulatory surgical services.[18] In the competition alternative the hospitals appear to have a distinct advantage. They already possess all the necessary equipment and personnel, but must rearrange their marketing mix to create a more pleasant, convenient environment, and deliver the product at a more competitive price. In regard to promotion, hospitals should "position" their advantages of comprehensive surgical backup, availability of immediate consultation and admission capabilities if needed.

For the private physician who performs minor surgery in his office, he can compete with the FASCs by promoting his own office "mini-surgical suite", positioning all the amenities associated with an office practice. The Combination Alternative offers some interesting possibilities. Hospitals can trade services with the FASCs by referring some of their ambulatory cases in "exchange" for referrals of more complicted surgical cases. If the exchange system is not feasible, offering 24 hour backup and comprehensive coverage for unexpected complications is a sensible means of negotiating with freestanding centers which will benefit both parties concerned.

Other Outpatient Adventures

The urgent care programs and the ambulatory surgery programs represent only two concepts on how to penetrate the general outpatient-ambulatory care market. Other interesting "adventures" might include establishing satellite clinics or emergency rooms in underserved areas, establishing "storefront offices" in key business areas or shopping districts, or establishing a program of mobile medical services to include either a mobile van or smaller vehicle capable of making "house calls" to restricted or otherwise "less accessible" patients. Each of these programs represent another opportunity for penetration of the general outpatient market. Each provider should weigh each possible option carefully, and only select those opportunities which meet his needs, are within his capabilities, and have the highest potential for successful market development.

Contract Negotiations

As the final category of general outpatient services, I have included this portion on contract negotiations. Although not a specific part of the outpatient program development synopsis, successful outpatient program development plays a very important role in potential contract negotiations by offering a lower cost alternative for medical care.

PPOs and other direct associations between employers, insurance companies and health care providers are rapidly advancing in the health care environment as insurers are seeking to find ways of reducing health care costs. Typical PPO arrangements have medical services delivered at a 15-25% discount. It is estimated that 40% of hospitals and private physicians already participate in contractual arrangements, trading "discounted" medical services for potential increases in patient volume.[34-36] As PPOs and contractual relationships proliferate, as more and more businesses and insurance companies seek medical care at lower costs, those health care providers that can deliver the more cost effective service packages will be in a more advantageous negotiation position to secure such contracts.

CONCLUSION

Some authors have predicted that "hospitals of the future will be ambulatory care centers and intensive care units, providing a limited range of services in between."[40]

Although outpatient revenues still represent only 15-20% of gross revenues for hospital services, the annual growth rate for these services has approached the 20% level.[41] A recent Blue Cross study revealed that there was an 18.6% decline in inpatient days, and a 137.6% increase in outpatient visits among Blue Cross subscribers between 1968 and 1978.[42] As trends continue to favor outpatient services to inpatient services, health care providers must be ready to make the adjustment.

The purpose of this paper was to highlight the changes in the health care environment as they relate to the outpatient-ambulatory market, and emphasize the need for traditional health care providers to react to the situation. The need for comprehensive market evaluation and situation analysis was stressed as being a necessary method for selecting only those opportunities most beneficial for the provider. A comprehensive model of opportunity analysis and strategy selection was presented to emphasize the point that each provider must go through a step by step decision process, unique to his own needs and capabilities before making the appropriate selection.

These are interesting times. Those providers who have the greatest foresight into the future and who develop the most innovative planning methods will do well when the "opportunity knocks." Be ready when it comes, and act accordingly, these are the keys to success.

REFERENCES

1. "The Changing Trends of Medical Care and its Impact on Traditional Providers: Adaptation and Survival via a Marketing Approach" A. Rosenstein MD, Health Marketing Quarterly Fall/1984 In Press.

2. "Non-traditional Revenue—Diversification for Profit" S.G. Kernaghan, Hosps. 12/1/82 p. 75-81.

3. "Strategies for a Crowded Marketplace" R.N. Clarke, L. Shyavitz, HCM Review Summer 1983 p. 45-51.

4. "Diversification—Broadening Hospital Services: What Makes Sense?" J. Goldsmith, Hosps. 12/1/82 p. 68-73.

5. "Blessings of a Doctor Surplus" B. Breining, Wall St. Journal 11/29/83.

6. "Marketing the Private Practice" E. Roberts, Ca. Health Rev. 12/83 p. 50.

7. Emergence—National Association of Freestanding Emergency Rooms publication, June-October 1983.

8. Emergency Centers Rise in the U.S." R. Heffler, LA Times 5/22/82 p. 29.

9. "Ambulatory Surgery" D. Detman et al., Surg. Clin. N.A. Vol. 62 no. 4 Aug. 1982 p. 685-704.

10. Consumerism: The Tables Are Turning" R.M. Cunningham Jr., Hosps. 3/1/81 p. 78-82.

11. "Entrepreneurship: Its Place in Health Care" J. Goldsmith, Hosp. Forum Vol. 27 Mar-Apr. 1984 p. 18-19.

12. "FECs Pose Competition for Hospital EDs" Glenn Richards, Hosps. 5/16/84 p. 77-82.

13. "Impact of FECs on Hospital ER Use" M. Ferber, Ann. Emer. Med. 7/83 p. 429-433.

14. "Slicing the Pie Thinner" E. Freidman, Hosps. 10/16/82 p. 62-74.

15. "Freestanding Centers Vie for Hospital Patients" J. Bendix, Mod. Health Care Jan. 1982 p. 1882.

16. Emergence—National Association of Freestanding Emergency Rooms publication, June-October 1983.

17. "...And Other Competition You'll Face in 1983" H. Eisenberg, Medical Economics 1/10/83 p. 239-248.

18. *Ambulatory Surgery* Linda Burns, Aspen publ. Rockville, Md. 1984 p. 7.

19. *Hospital Fact Book* 8th Ed. Ca. Hosp. Assoc. Sacramento, Ca. 1983 p. 39.

20. "The Content of Ambulatory Care in the U.S." R. Rosenblatt, D. Cherkin et al., NEJM 10/13/83 p. 892-897.

21. *Hospital Fact Book* California Hospital Association 1983 p. 38.

22. "Ambulatory Care—Can Hospitals Compete?" S. Williams, Hosp. and Hosp. Ad. Sept.-Oct./1983 p. 22-34.

23. "Trends and Initiatives in Hospital Ambulatory Care" L.A. Burns, Am. Jour. Hosp. Pharm. Vol. 39 May/1982 p. 799-805.

24. "The Ambulatory Response" D. Harris et al., Hosps. 5/16/83 p.69-71.

25. "Competition Spurs Ambulatory Choice" R. Gilbert, Hosps. 5/16/83 p. 67-68.

26. "Planning for Ambulatory Care Delivery Systems: A Market Segment Approach" D. Klegon, D. Gregory et al., HCM Rev. Vol. 7 Winter 1982 p. 35-45.

27. "Reflections on Change in Medical Practice. The Current Trend Toward Large Scale Medical Organizations" E. Saward et al., JAMA Vol. 250 no. 20 11/25/83 p. 2820-2825.

28. "Chrysler, Hit Hard by Medical Costs, Studies Health Care System" D. Rosenbaum N.Y. Times 3/15/84 p. 10.

29. "Why Acute Care Hospitals Must Undertake Long-Term Care" E. Campion, A. Bang, M. May, NEJM Vol. 308 no. 2 1/13/83 p. 71-75.

30. "The Increasing Supply of Physicians, The Changing Structure of the Health Services System, and the Future Practice of Medicine" A. Tarlov MD, NEJM Vol. 308 no. 20 5/19/83 p. 1235-1244.

31. "Current Controversy on Alternative Medicine" J. Lester, NEJM Vol. 309 no. 124 12/15/83 p. 1524-1527.

32. "Developing an Urgent Care Center" Amherst Asso. Inc. Seminar 2/27/84 San Francisco, Ca.

33. "Freestanding Centers Proliferate" Laurie Prothro, Hosp. Forum Vol. 26 May-June 1983 p. 21-22.

34. "Marketing the Private Practice" E. Roberts, Ca. Health Rev. 12/83 p. 50.

35. "PPO Activity in California Hospitals" C. White et al., Ca. Health Rev. Dec. 1983-Jan. 1984 p. 40-42.

36. "New Remedies" The Internist Nov.-Dec. 1983 p. 15-20.

37. "Competition—Getting a Fix on PPOs" K. Kodner, Hosps. 11/16/82 p. 59-66.
38. "Competition in the Health Care Marketplace" E. Melina et al., NEJM Vol. 308 no. 13 3/31/83 p. 788-792.
39. "Discount Medicine: Price Cutting Is in Vogue with Doctors, Hospitals" M. Waldholz, Wall St. Jour. 11/22/83 p. 1.
40. "The Ambulatory Response" D. Harris et al., Hosp. 5/16/83 p.69-71.
41. "Trends and Initiatives in Hospital Ambulatory Care" L.A. Burns, Am Jour. Hosp. Pharm. Vol. 39 May 1982 p. 799-805.
42. "Blue Cross Plans Experience Sharp 10 Year Decline in Hospital Utilization Rates" Blue Cross and Blue Shield Associations, 1/18/80.

SECTION TWO: STRATEGIES FOR SPECIFIC EXAMPLES OF AMBULATORY CARE SERVICES

As I mentioned in this issue's editorial, marketing strategies are the creative phase of health care marketing. The following articles provide some examples of marketing to different forms of ambulatory care. The reader may also want to refer to the editorial for strategy examples related to marketing urgent care centers or the next section for applications to pre-paid programs.

Marketing strategy development does not occur until the very end of a marketing plan. It is important to remember that these strategies are derived from the goals, objectives, marketing audit, analysis, and targeting work that has been developed before creating strategies. Marketing strategies are broad actions which the organization will implement to market to a select target(s) in order to satisfy the originally established marketing goals and objectives set up at the beginning of the planning process. Marketing tactics are differentiated from strategies by being the specific actions the organization will implement and are related to a specific strategy or strategies. For example, a marketing strategy would be the decision to implement a direct mail campaign for the service. A tactic related to this strategy would further describe it, such as sending out a two page letter by the administrator to all residents in the local community. In a marketing plan there can be many marketing strategies and tactics. However, the strategies and tactics are specifically interrelated to targets and goals and objectives of the marketing plan.

Many times marketing strategies can become the actual part of the marketing plan which is followed carefully as a 'cookbook' for marketing a service. In many instances, the marketing director will hand over the list of strategies and tactics to someone to start implementing without sharing all of the background material. I mention

51

this point because it is necessary to write these strategies and tactics very clearly and concisely within a marketing plan.

Marketing strategies can be developed in many different ways. Some simple basic points to always fall back on are to create strategies related to the four components of the marketing mix-pricing, place, product, and promotion. The first article in this section by Avram Kaplan clearly presents strategies applied to these components for emergency services. An alternative method is to develop strategies applicable to the phase of the life cycle in which the organization is in, whether it be the phase of Introduction, Growth, Maturity, or Decline. A service in each phase demands a unique mix of strategies.

This section demonstrates the applicability of marketing to a few ambulatory-related services. Even though a reader may be associated professionally with a select delivery mode, these articles may be helpful for their generic strategy development to the reader's service. Remember that marketing strategy development comes almost last in writing a marketing plan by following the lead of goals, objectives, audits, and targeting analysis.

WJW

Using the Components
of the Marketing Mix
to Market Emergency Services

Avram Kaplan

INTRODUCTION

One approach to marketing the emergency department is the use of the basic framework of the marketing mix. By definition the marketing mix consists of the service characteristics of product, place, price and promotion. Each component will be described and applied to developing marketing strategies for emergency department services. The sequence of the four "Ps" of the marketing mix as presented is no accident. This author believes we need to start with the product and end with promotion. The four Ps of marketing can always be used as a base from which to develop marketing strategies for any type of ambulatory service.

MARKETING MIX STRATEGIES

Product

The product is emergency service, a medical service attending to what the patient, our client, determines to be the clinical emergency. The patient determines what is an emergency, be it medical, surgical, psychiatric, or dental. Let's look at product characteristics of emergency care that are important if you want to successfully

Avram Kaplan, MPH, is Financial Analyst, Fischer Mangold, Inc., an emergency and ambulatory care contract service corporation, Pleasanton, California; Adjunct Professor, School of Health Services Management, Golden Gate University; formerly Center Director for the Emergency Department and Surgical Clinics at San Francisco General Hospital and Administrator, UCLA Emergency Department, Acute Care Clinic and Marion Davies Children's Clinic.

have people use the service. The fundamental characteristic is the provision of excellent clinical care by trained, skilled, experienced emergency physicians.

Look at the criteria for the foundation of your emergency department, the *emergency physician*:

—*Career Oriented*: Dedicated to emergency medicine
—*Full Time*: Emergency medicine practiced on a full time basis at the hospital; not a practice split up at different emergency departments, nor is the practice just a part time occupation.
—*Local, Live in Town*: Although the living distance from the hospital can be debated, the key is commitment and involvement in the local community and the hospital. The emergency physician should be known and respected by the community leaders and local physicians.
—*Clinically Competent, Experienced, Skilled Physician*: It is important to have experienced physicians in the emergency department; preferably emergency residency trained and emergency board certified or prepared. These credentials don't guarantee the clinical competency. Proctoring from the start of practice, a thorough reference check and ongoing peer review is absolutely necessary to ensure and verify the clinical abilities of the physician.
—*Sensitive, Personable, Caring Physician*: The cornerstone of Emergency Medicine is the clinical ability of the physician. However, patients, in my experience, evaluate medical service based on the art of communication, caring, respect for privacy, honest appraisal of the situation and if the physician is personable. A clinically competent, personable physician will probably derive better results and patient compliance. This physician will surely get fewer complaints.

The respect for the patients' time and physician charges, the awareness of the business side of medicine is important in these competitive and cost conscious times. Physicians should institute a differential pricing system. Minor, easily managed medical problems should be differentiated from more complex conditions. An example of this would be charging $25 for a minor sore throat exam to charging $200 for managing an overdosed patient.

Physicians should know how to use the various coding systems developed for professional fees, such as The Procedural Terminology for Emergency Medicine (PTEM), AN ADAPTATION OF CPT-4. The CPT-4 (Current Procedural Terminology-4th edition, AMA) is being adapted as a national standard of procedure coding for use by Medicare and is proposed for Medicaid. These coding schemes, and the still used California Standard Nomenclature (the old California Relative Value Studies or CRVS), provide an appropriate menu to select emergency professional fees. I will cover pricing in a later section, but it is clear that the physician can help to control medical costs, by differentiating their professional fees. In addition, an experienced emergency physician will know how to manage the emergency patient. This means having the ability to develop a differential diagnosis and treatment plan; ordering the most appropriate diagnostic tests, and prescribing the most cost effective clinical treatment plan. Furthermore, the experienced emergency physician knows how to ration the time given to each patient so as to efficiently move patients through the system. This reduced waiting time and improves room utilization.

Emergency Physicians are the key to the delivery of emergency services because they are the only ones licensed to practice medicine. Another part of this product is the emergency staff supporting and working with the physician. The nurses and other clinical staff must share the same characteristic of the physicians; clinical competency, skilled in the art of communication, personable in their treatment of the patient and aware of the business and finance issues. When I was the administrator of the UCLA Acute Care Clinic (a walk-in clinic), patients often replied favorably to the care received. Especially noted in favorable evaluations, were positive remarks about how the nurses and clerks treated the patients because they demonstrated a caring attitude.

The non-clinical staff: the registration clerks, cashiers, unit clerks and the volunteers are all a part of the team and their attitude and competency reflects on the whole Department. The emergency department is the window to the community for the hospital. How the patient and the patient's family are greeted and put through the business requirement of registration, can mean the difference between a satisfied customer and a dissatisfied one. The warm, caring demeanor of the registration clerk can set the stage for creating that "aura of welcome" that will stay and leave with the patient. With an average of 2-3 people accompanying each patient, think about the word of mouth referral from the patient and family/friends. Everybody is a potential client and everyone talks about their experience in the emergency department. The ultimate success of marketing is the referral.

The registration clerks have to elicit identification and payment information, often under conditions of considerable distress. These clerks should be well trained, experienced, competent professionals. Their skills should reflect human relations abilities, being able to work under stress and must be detail-oriented. In my analysis of evaluations from the UCLA Walk-In Clinic and Emergency Department, most complaints were derived from billing and waiting time problems. Setting up the billing arrangement correctly at the start of the encounter, avoids problems for the business office. Billing problems may surface after the medical care is given. These problems will reflect on the patient's experience. Having registration clerks who can gather correct billing data in a pleasant manner can minimize these problems.

The clinical staff: nurses, orderlies, Emergency Medical Technicians, paramedics, respiratory therapists, radiology technicians, etc. contribute to satisfactory outcome of care. This contribution includes the demonstration of a caring and personable attitude to the patient and patient's family. This attitude is important because the patient spends most of their time with these staff members. The physician director of the emergency department and nursing director should take the responsibility to set the tone of this caring environment.

In this section I have emphasized the product, but the product of clinical care is expanded to emphasizing the client's needs and expectations. Addressing what the patient perceives as "benefits" from their experience means creating a "service" environment that shows in the behavior of all of the emergency staff. This is what is called a marketing attitude. This means that you are tuned in to the patient's needs, and expectations, and that you will attempt to satisfy them. This is especially important because the majority of the patient's perceptions about the quality of the service comes from personal interaction with emergency personnel and the department's caring environment.

Place

Existing emergency departments can't choose their location, but this category of place means more than physical location. "Place" focuses on service hours, access, and parking. Consider this checklist.

—*Hours*: Emergency medicine has always been known as the Department of Available Medicine. This is not an issue; the emergency department is always open.

—*Telephone*: A well publicized public phone number so that patients may call for directions on how to get to the facility should also be coupled with a TTY type phone for the deaf.

—*Access*: Separate walk-in entrance from the ambulance entrance so as not to hinder the arrival and unloading of patients from the ambulance.

—*Signage*: Clear, adequate signage from within the hospital and externally, including lighted street signs.

—*Parking*: Close parking access. Make it convenient for the patient and the handicapped.

—*Waiting Area*: Warm, comfortable seating arrangements, allowing for cluster seating (families often come with a patient); Television to help the time go by; magazines, other reading materials; coffee and vending machines nearby; and a volunteer offering coffee or tea to visitors is well received.

—*Public Transportation*: Making available public transit information, such as maps, time tables, designated phone for taxi service and other information to make it convenient for the patient to leave and get to the emergency department.

The foundation of addressing the place component is making it easy for the patient to get to the facility.

Price

Price competition is relatively new to physician services, but it is a growing practice. Emergency physicians have a long history of charging a fair price for the service rendered. The use of the fee schedule, such as the CRVS or CPT-4, allows for a charging practice that reflects the service rendered. Minor medical problems are charged relatively lower than major problems that require more time and skill. Emergency physicians, in effect, *tier* their prices.

Emergency departments frequently have not tiered the facility fees, but instead still charge a flat fee per visit (or there might be two or three fee levels). By tiering the facility fee, which must reflect the intensity of service delivered, the emergency department can be price competitive.

For minor medical problems, the facility fee could be $23 and the corresponding physician fee could be $23; for a total of $46. This is a fee that competes against freestanding urgent care centers, yet it is not so low as to compete against the private medical staff. There should be criteria set as to what patient's medical conditions should fit in this "convenience track" category, so there is no confusion in charging practices and in promoting this tiered and competitive pricing. An example of a patient who is put into the convenience track is one who comes in with a cold or minor sore throat. They are charged a set base facility and professional fee that is competitive with urgent care centers.

Promotion

That promotion comes at the end of the four "Ps" is no mistake. For many people, promotion is synonymous with marketing, but promotion is only a part of marketing strategy and really can only be used if there is a sound product to promote.

Promotion in health care has been low-key. Often this has been demonstrated by a simple listing of the hospital or physician in the yellow pages which highlight their services and credentials. In the more competitive marketplace, hospitals and physicians are trying more aggressive promotional strategies. In marketing the emergency department there are some strategies that can be used successfully. It is suggested that an organized marketing plan be developed before implementing any of the following strategies.

1. *Health education pamphlets in the waiting room*: All pamphlets should have the hospital logo and identification clearly imprinted on the cover. Where there is a need for multi-lingual communication; written material should be translated in the appropriate languages. Topics should be pertinent to medical problems seen in the emergency department and prevention of illnesses and disease.

2. *In-house tours of the emergency department*: At UCLA I brought in elementary children on a tour of the Emergency Department, but more importantly, they had a chance to talk to a nurse, physician and paramedic, in one of our classrooms. The purpose of this tour was to alleviate fear of these "people in white"; to understand how they would be taken care of in case of an emergency (they even walked through an ambulance) and to remember that "we care" at the UCLA Emergency Department. The children went home with the

"UCLA Emergency Department" clothing/belongings bag which we used for patients. At another hospital in Ohio, a similar tour program called "Operation Big Band Aid" is an example of the same strategy.

3. *Community Disaster Drills*: At UCLA we had Boy Scouts act as mock accident victims for our disaster drills. These drills were quite realistic and involved other organizations, such as the fire department, ambulance companies and the police. We staged a disaster drill and a community awareness open house which included rescue demonstrations by a variety of agencies. This event received television coverage and attracted over 500 people to the demonstration.

4. *Emergency Department Open House*: For example, at the UCLA Emergency Department when the new critical care monitoring and treatment room opened, we staged an open house for the hospital employees and medical staff. The target groups could be expanded to include pre-hospital care personnel, civic leaders, facility and other community representatives.

5. *Public Speaking*: This can take many forms including: luncheon speaking, guest lecturing, panel discussions, question and answer sessions and formal speeches. Suggested topics could be first aid, citizen cardiopulmonary respiration, use of emergency services, and prevention of on the job emergencies. Target groups can be: the elderly—social clubs, church, recreational centers; churches; industry; work and social clubs—Rotarian, Chamber of Commerce, etc.; schools.

6. *Convenience of Service*: This is a real perceived benefit by the patient. The convenience track, a speedier, less costly service to patients with certain minor problems can be promoted. This is done by a number of hospitals in answer to competition from freestanding urgent care centers. One caution: If you offer the service, you must deliver the product and be specific on medical criteria that puts the patient in the convenience track. I have seen the criteria set so that about 10% of the patients fall into this category. One example of how this service has been promoted is where a hospital has placed advertisements in newspapers announcing the 35% reduction in price for the care of minor medical problems seen in the emergency department. This is a competitive tactic aimed at the urgent care center located one block away.

7. *Promotion Through the Use of Brochures*: A brochure describing the emergency department; providing information on location, phone number, credentials, special programs and the uniqueness of your services, can be mailed to target groups. These include:
   a. industry
   b. civic groups
   c. Chamber of Commerce
   d. hotels and motels
   e. camp grounds
   f. trailer parks
   g. all the housing in the area (particularly families and the elderly)
   h. medical staff and other physicians in the community.
   i. fire and police departments
   j. private ambulances
   k. charitable organizations
   l. religious institutions and facilities
   m. Boy Scouts, Girl Scouts, etc.
   n. fraternal organizations
   o. schools
   p. Welcome Wagon
   q. public utilities (especially the telephone company)
   r. local military bases
   s. other health and human service organizations in the community

   The brochure could include some items that will "tickle" the memory of a potential patient to use your services such as:

   —At least two telephone stickers highlighting emergency ambulance, police, fire numbers, but identifying the hospital emergency department.
   —Four registration and medical data cards to be sent back to the emergency department for use as a ready reference to speed registration (all data must still be verified at the time of registration).
   —Two consent to treat minor cards, to be returned to the emergency department to keep on file and one for home reference.

   The brochure should be professionally designed and written as it reflects the professionalism of the hospital. This should include the brochure being attention getting, clearly written to avoid technical medical jargon and useful as a reference.

8. *Having the Physicians Telephone Patients, at Home, After They Receive Care*: Making a follow up phone call, to selected patients, is an exhilarating experience for the patient and the physician. Most patients don't expect a physician to call them, ever; so patients who receive a follow up call are very often pleased and appreciative and remember the *special care* shown them. Physicians who have made such calls often express how pleased they are at the response they get.

9. *Promotion Through Providing Education and Feedback to Ambulance Personnel*: This can be effective in ensuring that they will remember where to bring cases—to the people who treat them with dignity and professionalism.

10. *Networking*: Establishing relationships with other human and health service organizations to obtain referrals. Examples of these organizations are: United Way; Family Service Agency; Planned Parenthood; talk-lines; crisis lines; long term care agencies; mental health programs; hospitals without emergency departments; urgent care centers; preferred provider organizations; industrial clinics; medical information directories.

11. *Physicians in the Community and Medical Staff at the Hospital*: Private physicians respond to the excellence of clinical care, appropriateness of referrals and consultation requests and, if the emergency physicians, respect the bond of the patient in the private physician-patient relationship.

These eleven basic marketing strategies are only a sample of the many available promotional tactics for the emergency department. It is hoped that some are applicable to your needs. We, at the Fisher Mangold Group, believe the key to success in marketing emergency department services is having an organized marketing plan and a commitment to quality service.

SUMMARY

The preceding review of marketing strategies has been based on this author's extensive experience in ambulatory care management. It is hoped that the reader has obtained an understanding of the following:

1. Theoretical concept of the marketing mix.
2. The importance of sequencing in using the components of the marketing mix (4Ps).
3. The specific programmatic applications of these marketing mix components to emergency department services.
4. Specific tactics that the reader can use in marketing their emergency department service and/or other ambulatory care services.

REFERENCES

Text:

Marketing Health Care by Robin E. MacStravic, Aspen Systems, Inc., Germantown, Maryland, 1977.

Periodicals:

Health Marketing Quarterly, edited by William J. Winston, The Haworth Press, New York, 1984, Vol. I, Issues 1 & 2.
The Journal of Ambulatory Care Management; Aspen Systems Corporation, Rockville, Maryland, 1981.

Marketing Strategies
for an Ambulatory Geriatric
Health Care Program

Lynette M. Loomis

INTRODUCTION

Medical model geriatric day care centers provide medical supervision, rehabilitative therapies, and socialization opportunities to ambulatory but disabled or infirm adults. Such programs enable adults to delay or avoid institutionalization, thereby maintaining important family and community support systems.

The scope of care provided by staff is far more extensive than that which family caregivers are able to provide. Day programs also provide family caregivers with the respite and peace of mind needed to maintain jobs, household routines or the pursuit of recreational or educational activities. In many instances, the cost of day care is less than the cost of institutional placement, with cost savings estimates ranging from 12% to 68% of nursing home or hospitalization costs.

In the continuum of ambulatory geriatric health care outlined by Weiler and Rathbone-McCuan (see Table 1), there are four levels of care. The basic level provides socialization to socially regressed individuals. The highest level of care provides medical care and supervision to people recovering from an acute illness. St. John's Home, a 473-bed multi-level geriatric health-care facility in Rochester, New York, developed Day Break—Monroe County's first geriatric day care center—in 1975. In the continuum of geriatric day services, Day Break is considered a social/health center. In terms of New York State's Public Health Law, Day Break is a "medical model" day care program. In this medical model program, a registered nurse supervises the program, emergency medical care

---

Lynette M. Loomis, MA, MBA, is Director of Marketing and Communication at St. John's Home, Rochester, New York.

TABLE 1
GERIATRIC DAY SERVICES

Modality	Major Service Objective	Type of Client	Service Setting
Day hospital	To provide daily medical care and supervision to help the individual regain an optimal level of health following an acute illness	Individual is in active phase of recovering from an acute illness, no longer requiring intense medical intervention on a periodic basis	Extended care facility or hospital
Social/ health center	To provide health care resources when required to chronically impaired individuals	Individual has chronic physical illness or disabilities; condition does not require daily medical intervention but does require nursing and other health supports	Long-term care institution or free-standing center
Psycho-social center	To provide a protective or transitional environment that assists the individual in dealing with multiple problems of daily coping	Individual has a history of psychiatric disorder; could reactivate and/or suffer from mental deterioration (organic or functional) that places him in danger if he is not closely supervised	Psychiatric institution or free-standing center
Social center	To provide appropriate socialization services	Individual's social functioning has regressed to the point where, without formal, organized social stimuli, overall capacity for independent functioning would not be possible	Specialized senior citizen center

[1]Philip G. Weiler and Eloise Rathbone-McCuan, *Adult Day Care: Community Work With the Elderly* (New York: Springer Publishing Company, 1978), p. 7.

is provided by the Home's full-time physicians, occupational, physical and speech therapies are provided as medically indicated, and recreational programs are provided daily.

Day Break is financed through fees for service. Medicaid authorizes reimbursement for this service and private pay clients are also accepted. A sliding fee scale has been in place since the program's beginning, and the local United Way has made small grants upon occasion to offset program deficits resulting from sliding scale usage. The United Way Allocations Committee has stressed the importance of maintaining a breakeven budget and reducing financial dependence on outside resources.

In 1983, Day Break's program director expressed concern that actual program census was 15% to 20% below projected census (Table 2). It was believed that a significant financial deficit would occur if this pattern continued. Marketing staff determined that an audit was indicated for two reasons: (1) to determine the basis for decreased attendance and gain a marketplace perspective of the program and (2) to demonstrate the role of marketing in health care to staff and the board of directors.

THE AUDIT

The marketing audit was conducted over a nine-month period. Staff reviewed local and state demographics and county population projections. Admissions data for a five-year period were analyzed, a client profile was developed, and a literature search of ambulatory health programs for the aged was conducted. A comparative program analysis included other ambulatory care programs and Day Break's competitive position was assessed. The program's promotional efforts were reviewed and the financial feasibility of the program was studied.

Nineteen mentally able Day Break participants, 26 family caregivers and 22 referral sources were surveyed in order to better understand the program's image. The survey consisted of rank order items, a three-point Likert scale rating satisfaction, and open-ended questions. Survey questions included reasons for investigating day programs and selecting Day Break, alternatives considered, and the degree to which the program conformed with expectations. The survey administered to referral sources also included questions pertaining to admissions criteria, processing of referrals, reasons cited by potential clients for refusing to attend the program and suggestions for expanding program services.

The audit identified several areas warranting investigation and action:

(1) Day Break was in the decline phase of the product life cycle. A major advantage enjoyed by the program in the mid-70s was the

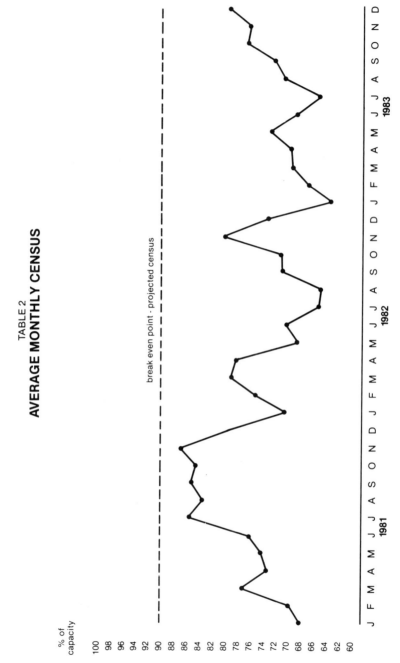

TABLE 2
AVERAGE MONTHLY CENSUS

lack of competition. Since that time, four programs have been developed within the community and a fifth is being planned.

(2) Admissions were lower than the level needed to bring program census to the break even point. Only 35% to 43% of the clients referred to Day Break over the two years previous to the audit were admitted to the program (Table 3). Referrals deemed inappropriate included those in which the potential client needed more medical supervision or personal care than could be provided. Those included referrals of people who were incontinent, required feeding or who wandered. Some applicants who were appropriate for the program refused to participate and expressed concern that Day Break was "one step away from being in a nursing home." Other reasons cited for failure to participate included lack of transportation or funds, or the individual's discomfort in group settings.

(3) Attendance patterns did not facilitate a daily census nearing the break even point. More than half of all Day Break clients attended the program two or three days a week and another 20% attended all five days a week. Reimbursement, based on attendance, varied from day to day.

(4) Absenteeism was a common occurrence in this population group. Illness, inclement weather, lack of transportation, physician appointments and family vacations created frequent fluctuations in program census.

(5) Marketing efforts had been directed to the end users of Day Break—the potential clients. Survey results showed that Day Break clients, regardless of mental ability, were usually not the primary

TABLE 3
ADMISSIONS DATA 1981 & 1982

	1981	1982
Referrals	108	105
Admissions	46 (43%)	37 (35%)
Rejections due to health	21 (19%)	17 (16%)
Refusals to participate	21 (19%)	20 (19%)
Referrals which were not followed thru	14 (13%)	24 (23%)
Other	6 (6%)	7 (7%)
Total	100%	100%

rounded to nearest per cent

decision makers. Family caregivers assessed several options and discussed their choice with the potential service user. Despite Day Break's certification as a medical model program, medical concerns and the availability of rehabilitative therapies were not the primary reasons cited by caregivers for selecting a day program.

(6) Referral sources sought ambulatory care programs for people whose disabilities were greater than those who, because of staffing patterns and physical space, could be accommodated by Day Break.

(7) Referral sources expressed frustration with the lack of easily accessible, affordable transportation to service sites. Day Break did not provide transportation, and client disabilities prohibited the practical use of public transportation. Family cars were not reasonable options for clients in wheelchairs.

(8) Day Break did not have a clearly defined positioning strategy. Although generic brochures were kept current, and staff were always available to address professional groups, no concerted marketing effort had been conducted since the program's development in the 1970s. The number of inappropriate referrals received and responses to open-ended survey questions indicated that Day Break was not easily distinguished from other ambulatory care programs. Thirty-nine percent of the clients, 44% of the family caregivers, and 53% of the referral sources cited the reputation of St. John's Home as one of the three most important reasons for selecting Day Break, rather than a specific program feature.

DEVELOPMENT OF MARKETING STRATEGIES

Results of the marketing audit prompted several decisions. The most important decision was to continue the program while launching a marketing effort aimed at increasing program census. Although referral sources indicated an increasing need for ambulatory care programs at a higher level of care than provided by Day Break, neither the financial nor physical plant resources existed to move or expand program services. Staff also felt that Day Break was an important part of the community's continuum of geriatric health care and that census could be increased appreciably by a concerted marketing effort.

An overall positioning strategy for Day Break was developed. That strategy was to position the program as part of a community-oriented continuum of geriatric health care of high quality at a median price for adults with moderate physical and/or psychological disabilities in need of some combination of medical supervision, recreation and socialization in an ambulatory care setting.

A creative strategy was developed which included the portrayal of at least one man or woman using an assistive device, such as a walker or wheelchair, in all promotional materials. The strategy also specified that minority members were to be represented in all printed materials and that all copy would be closed with an invitation to visit the program.

Public relations strategies included the identification of Day Break as a specific entry in the area's Yellow Pages and a telephone hot-line and referral service, separate from that of St. John's Home. Quarterly objectives were established for the submission of human interest stories about the program and its participants to area newspapers.

A major focus of the pricing strategy was an increase in program fees to more adequately reflect the true cost of service. The sliding fee scale was maintained and a goal was set to develop more specific criteria by which to determine fee scale eligibility.

POSITIONING STRATEGIES FOR TARGET MARKETS

A major thrust of the marketing plan was the identification of target markets and a better understanding of their needs. Through the interpretation of survey data and personal contacts six major segments were identified as warranting specific positioning strategies.

Physicians and medical discharge planners—this is the largest target market and is potentially the most easily accessed. Although target physicians are easily identified through their medical specialty, they are difficult to motivate to investigate geriatric day care as an appropriate resource for their patients. Physicians are concerned with the ongoing medical care of potential Day Break participants or may refer to the program for the respite it affords adult caregivers. Major benefits sought are rehabilitative therapies and medical supervision.

Strategy—position Day Break as a medical model day care program which provides care of high quality, effective occupational and physical therapy, and reliable medical supervision, and which consistently provides informative feedback to the referring professional.

Community agency personnel—is one of two segments which ranks number two in order of priority. This segment is more difficult to identify as members are employed in a wide variety of agencies in which employment turnover can affect the number of incoming referrals. This segment seeks to maintain adults at the lowest level of appropriate care while providing family caregivers with a sense of relief and security. Ongoing financial support for many of these agencies is sometimes partially based on the number of referral services provided.

Strategy—position Day Break as a program which is responsive to the community and is sensitive to the needs of families struggling with the demands of ongoing home care.

Adult caregivers—also ranks second in order of importance. This group seeks relief from the home care of an older or disabled family member. Caregivers also seek care options which provide them with a sense of security and a reduction in the guilt many of them feel from being unable to provide total care for a family member.

Strategy—position Day Break as an extension of the family caregiver unit—concerned, friendly, sensitive to individual needs and 100% reliable.

County referral agency—has been isolated from other community agencies as the mission of this organization deals specifically with the coordination of services for individuals remaining in the community or who require intermediate services while awaiting residential placement. Referral realization and facilitation of the case management function are major benefits sought by this group.

Strategy—position Day Break as a dependable referral recipient which is prompt in responding to family caregivers upon receipt of a referral and which is prompt in providing feedback to referral sources. An additional component in this strategy is the concept that St. John's rehabilitative therapists seek to move adults to their highest level of functioning.

Area clergy—is the smallest of the significant target markets. Clergy are often the only professional resource consulted by a family whose older or disabled relative is in need of professional care. Benefits sought by this group include perpetuation of clergy's ability to be informed and helpful resource people. Clergy also seek assistance in helping family members deal with feelings of doubt surrounding the decision to seek community resources.

Strategy—position Day Break as a community resource which

will take extra time to work with families around their ambivalence regarding daytime placement of a loved one and to reassure family caregivers that their decision has been a good one.

Potential Day Break participants—not the most significant target market. The decision to investigate the program is made by the family caregiver on behalf of the person in need. The mentally capable adult may have a major part in the final decision about participation and is the person most influential in deciding to remain in the program. Post-enrollment satisfaction, rather than the initial decision making process, is a key issue with this segment.

Strategy—position Day Break as a place in which participants can meet people just like themselves—friends who can relate to their interests, memories and concerns for the future. An additional concept is the personal interest Day Break staff members take in each and every client.

In addition to the general strategies outlined above, specific goals were established for each target group accompanied by strategies and budget guidelines. Table 4 depicts sample goals and strategies.

PROGRESS TO DATE

Implementation of Phase I of the marketing plan commenced in the first quarter of 1984. This included solicitation from the local United Way for deficit funding by which to maintain the program as staff worked to increase program census. Targeted mailings of a professional's brochure were processed. Family caregivers have received two written quarterly program reports including feedback on the client's health and social relationships.

The St. John's Home Speaker's Bureau was launched and has addressed more than 300 professionals and community members. Each speaking engagement has provided staff an opportunity to talk about ambulatory care at St. John's Home and to distribute Day Break brochures. Day Break staff collaborated with another medical model day program in the development of an eight-week seminar entitled "As Families Grow Older." This educational symposium was targeted to family caregivers of older or disabled adults who are not enrolled in a day program.

One area which has been identified as in need of further improvement is the identification of the original referral source. Although program staff have been diligently asking family caregivers and cli-

TABLE 4
Sample Marketing Goals and Strategies for Target Segments

Segment	Goal	Strategy
Physicians & Medical Personnel	Increase medical referrals to 50% of all referrals	• Forward 700 Professionals Guide with cover letter from medical director to physicians, and 200 guides to identified medical personnel. Increase references to Day Break at Medical Society meetings.
Community Agency Personnel	Decrease number of unrealized referrals by 15%.	• Inform referral sources of fee increase while reminding them of sliding fee scale option.
Family Caregivers	Increase level of satisfaction with "level of information shared" to a 75% response rate in the "better than expected" category.	• Develop brochure which reinforces services which enhance their caregiving. Forward list of daily activities on a monthly basis.
County Referral Agency	Increase proportion of realized referrals to 50%.	• Develop check list of acceptance criteria to enable referral sources to predetermine appropriateness of referral and a referral response packet by which to provide prompt disposition information.
Clergy	Increase referrals to 5% of total referrals.	• Forward 600 Professionals Guide with cover letter from Board president (a pastor). • Invite area congregations within 5 miles of Day Break to receive Newsletter.
Participants	Maintain current overall level of satisfaction at 80% response rate for "better than expected" in satisfaction survey.	• Assign willing Day Break participants task of greeting newcomers and describing program.

ents how they first learned about Day Break, as many as one-third reply "family" or "friends." Marketing staff will be working with program staff on interview techniques by which to pursue more specific information. This will be helpful in determining the appropriateness of the marketing strategies and their impact.

Both program and marketing staff are encouraged by the increase in the program census thus far this year. Average daily census in the first five months of 1984 increased 16% over the same time frame in the previous year and was 13% higher than the year end average of 1983. As other phases of the marketing plan are implemented, it is hoped that the strategies selected will prove to be the correct ones. The overall goal is that program census will rise another 5% to reach the break even point and continue until maximum capacity is reached.

SUMMARY

Ambulatory programs for elderly or disabled adults require concerted marketing efforts. Potential participants are rarely the individuals who make the decision to participate and therefore rely on information and recommendations of medical and community referral sources and family members. The nature of the physical and mental disabilities of the client population and the deteriorating nature of some of their health problems result in frequent absenteeism and termination of service. For these reasons, generic marketing strategies are less successful than marketing efforts directed at specific target groups who, despite such similarities as "medical professionals" or "community agencies," seek different benefits from ambulatory care centers.

REFERENCES

1. Linda Aaronson, "Adult Day Care: A Developing Concept," *Journal of Gerontological Social Work*, Vol. 5(3), Spring 1983, pp. 35-47.
2. Renato Pablo and Fran Cleary, "Parkwood Day Hospital: An Alternative for the Impaired Elderly," *Canadian Journal of Public Health*, Vol. 73(3), May/June 1982, pp. 176-182.
3. William Weissert, "Two Models of Geriatric Day Care: Findings from a Comparative Study, *The Gerontologist*, Vol. 16, 1976, pp. 420-427.

Fitness and Health Promotion: Big Business and Good Business in Dallas "What, Where, Why, and How"

Sheryl H. Boyd

The health status of America's chief resource, her citizens, has become an issue of national concern. With costs in the health-care industry (the nation's second largest) escalating to $340 billion (10.5% of the GNP in 1983, $1300 per capita), insurers, employers, providers, citizens, and the government recognize that WELLNESS is an important goal—economically, medically, managerially, and socially. As Will Durant said, "The health of nations is more important than the wealth of nations." Also, President Reagan in a spring 1984 address to the Health Insurance Association of America charged that: "America can only be as strong and healthy as its people, and, as in all things, the only lasting change that takes place comes when each of us does his part to make our country the good and decent place we want it to be."

The goal of greater wellness for the majority of American citizens presents a collective challenge for managers, medical personnel, and marketers. In this paper, the findings of a two-part survey conducted in Dallas, Texas in spring 1984 which addressed the corporate viewpoint toward health promotion and assessed local fitness facility programs will be reviewed.

Sheryl H. Boyd, EdD, is Assistant Professor and Director of the Health Services MBA Program in The Graduate School of Management, University of Dallas, Irving, Texas. Dr. Boyd holds a BS in Education from Capital University, Columbus, Ohio, and earned her MBA in Management and EdD in Higher Education at Texas Tech University, Lubbock, Texas. Special recognition is extended to Stephen O'Connor, Wayne Hansen, and Michelle Stone for their research assistance with this study.

INTRODUCTION

Wellness must be viewed as a kind of robustness that comprehends respect for the total body and an appreciation of its worth—a positive well-being physically, emotionally, mentally, and socially. The attainment of wellness includes a continuum of activities: medical care, disease prevention, health education, worksite safety, and total body fitness. The goal of fitness and health promotion programs is to help people understand that what they do for themselves and to themselves can have as equally powerful an influence on their health status as can the major medical and technological advances of the 20th century.

Traditionally, Americans have enjoyed the right to eat, drink, or smoke themselves to death and employers have not interfered with these behaviors. However, in the past ten years the trend for employer promotion of health fitness has gained momentum. Employers now recognize and medical claims support the fact that one of an executive's biggest occupational hazards may be his desk and swivel chair. Working in a typically designed modern office or automated factory setting requires expending less physical exertion than does taking a hot shower. Sedentary work requirements allow systems, especially the muscular, respiratory, and cardiovascular, to degenerate. This combination of inactivity and overconsumption often results in major health problems. Hence, personal involvement in fitness and wellness programs can be viewed as a "rust-proofing" system that protects a person from life's rat races of appointments, meetings, business entertaining, and other morning-to-night stressors. Employers are in a position to provide leadership in this area because the majority of working people spend about half their waking hours at the worksite.

Further, the wellness movement's expanding popularity has been fueled by a growing understanding of the costs attributable to lifestyle-related illnesses (heart attacks, cancer, accidents, and cirrhosis). For employers, as a major purchaser of health benefits, the medical costs associated with lifestyle-related illnesses are further multiplied through their impact on absenteeism, productivity, disability, workman's compensation, turnover, retraining, reduced morale, and retiree benefits.

Recognizing that wellness programs can be developed for any size and type of company through a variety of community-based or on-site approaches, this study was designed to assess the state of the art regarding employer health promotion and fitness/wellness offerings in Dallas, Texas. Due to the continuing influx of new corporate headquarters followed by a rapidly growing work force in the past decade, the marketplace for community-based wellness opportunities in Dallas has experienced rapid expansion. Section I of this study summarizes the community-based fitness/wellness program survey findings. Hopefully, this data will provide useful guidelines for employers, individuals, and fitness program managers in the design, selection, marketing, or evaluation of fitness/health promotion activities.

COMMUNITY-BASED FITNESS CENTER/WELLNESS PROGRAM SURVEY

In this the year of the Olympics, the opportunity to survey and study fitness and wellness programs available to Dallas employers, employees, and other citizens presented an exciting challenge. To conduct this study, a 37-question survey instrument was designed. This questionnaire was divided into four major categories to collect data regarding facility, consumer, medical and recreational, and promotional characteristics on each center. This comprehensive instrument was mailed to the Executive Directors of each of the 75 fitness centers currently identified as operational in Dallas County. Completed questionnaires were returned by 53% of these centers.

It should be noted that the participants in this study represent a variety of types of fitness centers. The sponsorship of the programs ranged from hospital based, to Cooper's Aerobics Center, to YMCAs, to commercially franchised fitness clubs. However, though there exists a variety of fitness/wellness center types operational in Dallas, each of the questionnaire categories was answered by all but a few of the respondents. Also, as questionnaire replies were tabulated, it became apparent that respondents checked more than one answer in many of the multi-variable questions. Hence, for those questions, each response choice must be viewed as an independent variable and compared only to the 100% of total responses for that particular question. Due to the length of the questionnaire, the findings are presented in Figure 1.

1. WHEN DID YOUR FACILITY OPEN AND WHAT IS ITS SIZE?

    1885 DALLAS YMCA

5 Between 1885-1969 - 12.5%	Largest	120,000 Square Feet
10 Between 1970-1979 - 25.0%	Smallest	1,000 Square Feet
25 Between 1980-1984 - 62.5%	Average	23,328 Square Feet

2. WHAT IS THE FORM OF OWNERSHIP OF YOUR FACILITY?

Corporate	46.2%	Hospital	5.1%
Partnership	15.4%	Church	2.6%
Sole Proprietorship	15.4%	Franchise	2.6%
Non-Profit	10.3%	Subsidiary	2.6%

3. IS OR WAS YOUR FACILITY SUBSIDIZED BY ANY OF THE FOLLOWING?

Bank Loans	46.0%	Government Grants	7.7%
Corporate Donations	25.6%	Bonds	2.6%
Private Donations	25.6%	Insurance Company	2.6%
United Way	10.3%	Personal Money	2.6%

4. DO YOU HAVE ANY ADDITIONAL PLANS FOR NEW FACILITIES OR

    SERVICES IN THE NEAR FUTURE?

Yes	81.6%	No	18.4%
New	76.3%		
Expanded	23.7%		

5. INDICATE THE TYPES AND AMOUNTS OF INSURANCE CARRIED TO

    PROTECT YOUR CLIENTS.

Liability	82%	Doctor's Own Liability	5%
Comprehensive	51%	Liability for Childen	5%
Malpractice	5%	Hospital Umbrella Policy	5%

6. DOES YOUR FACILITY HAVE ADVANCED LIFE SUPPORT EQUIPMENT?

No	79.5%	(Includes: Emergency Cart, Oxygen,
Yes	12.8%	Defibrillator, EKG, Drug Box,
No Response	7.7%	Suction, Ventilation Equipment,
		Crash Cart)

7. WHAT IS YOUR FACILITY'S DISTANCE FROM THE NEAREST HOSPITAL?

Less Than One Mile	11%
1 - 5 Miles	78%
Greater Than 5 Miles	11%

8. WHAT ARE YOUR FACILITY'S HOURS OF OPERATION?

    Hours Vary From 8-Hour To 24-Hour Shifts

9. INDICATE THE ANNUAL FEE FOR THE FOLLOWING TYPES OF

    MEMBERSHIPS:

	Individual	Family	Corporate
Range	$175 - $1,380	$175 - $1,560	$282 - $1,560
Average	$372	$557	$567

FIGURE 1.

10. TOTAL MEMBERSHIP:

	1980	1981	1982	1983
Range	75 - 4,971	75 - 6,321	50 - 6,049	50 - 6,000
Average	1,924	1,763	1,737	1,783

11. WHICH OF THE FOLLOWING PAYMENT PLANS DOES YOUR FACILITY OFFER?

Monthly Payments	71%	Employee Deduction	71%
Special Introductory	45%	Time Payments	21%
Bank Drafts	40%	Quarterly Payments	16%

Other: Charge Cards, Pay-As-You-Go, Up-Front One-Year Payment, Discount For Registering One Week In Advance, Semi-Annual, Pay Eleven Months - Get 12 Months.

12. WHICH OF THE FOLLOWING ARE OFFERED AT YOUR FACILITY?

Listed In Order Of Highest Reported Frequency:

Exercise Room	Jogging Track	Treadmill
Weight Room	Pool	Racquetball Courts
Sauna	Steambath	Self-Defense
Whirlpool	Classrooms	Teaching Kitchen
		Tennis Courts

Other: Aerobics, Hairstyling Salon, Inhalation Room, Massage, Sunbed, Cold Plunger, Squash, Gym, Softball Field, 3-Hole Golf, Obstacle Course, Private Rooms, Dance Studio, Playground Area, Fencing.

13. DOES YOUR FACILITY OFFER ANY OF THE FOLLOWING?

Child Day-Care	61.5%	Snackbar	28.6%
Towel Service,		Game Room,	
Vending Machines	46.2%	Restaurant	12.8%
Shop	38.5%	Library	7.7%
Lounge, Personal Grooming	33.3%	Elementary Day Care	5.1%

14. INDICATE THE NUMBER OF PEOPLE EMPLOYED BY YOUR FACILITY:

	Full Time	Part Time	Consultants
Range	1 - 140	1 - 50	1 - 10
Average	27	15	4

15. INDICATE THE HIGHEST LEVEL OF EDUCATION ACHIEVED AND THE NUMBER OF EMPLOYEES WHO HAVE ACHIEVED IT:

Bachelor Degree	47.2%	Master Degree	7.2%
High School	23.1%	Doctorate Degree	4.5%
Certificate	14.1%	Associate Degree	3.9%

16. DOES YOUR FACILITY PROVIDE MONETARY REIMBURSEMENT FOR CONTINUING EDUCATION OF EMPLOYEES?

No	59.0%
Yes	35.9%
No Response	5.1%

FIGURE 1 (continued)

17. WHAT PRODUCTS DOES YOUR FACILITY HAVE FOR SALE?

    Listed In Order Of Highest Reported Frequency:

    T-Shirts, Dancewear, Rackets, Workout Clothes, Nutrition
    Diet Plan, Personal Items, Sporting Goods, Gloves, Food,
    Beverages, Eye Guards, Weight Equipment, Shoe Laces,
    Clothing, Vitamins, Shoes, Socks, Used Exercise Equipment,
    Eye Goggles, Tote Bags, Tanning Goggles, Nutritional
    Products, Sanitary Items, Activewear.

18. WHAT PERCENTAGE OF CLIENTELE ARE:

	Male	Female
Range	10% - 100%	6% - 100%
Average	39%	62%

19. WHAT PERCENTAGE OF YOUR CLIENTELE ARE:

	Under 20	21-40 Years	41-60 Years	Over 60
Range	3% - 75%	20% - 100%	4% - 90%	1.4% - 15%
Average	18.5%	61.5%	24.9%	9%

20. WHAT PERCENTAGE OF YOUR CLIENTELE ARE:

	Range	Average
Professionals	23% - 100%	71.8%
Unskilled	8% - 85%	28.5%
Other: Students, Military, Children	10% - 75%	25.4%
Retired	1% - 20%	9.4%
Not Working	1% - 50%	9.5%

21. WHAT PERCENTAGE OF THE MEMBERSHIP RETAINS MEMBERSHIP FOR:

	Over 2 Years	1-2 Years	1 Year	Under 1 Year
Range	5% - 90%	5% - 50%	5% - 96%	4% - 80%
Average	42.7%	29.3%	30.9%	30.1%

22. WHAT PERCENTAGE OF YOUR CLIENTELE COMMUTES FROM A DISTANCE

    OF:

1 - 5 Miles	66.8%	10 - 15 Miles	29.3%
5 - 10 Miles	28.1%	Over 15 Miles	4.0%

23. WHAT TIME OF DAY IS YOUR FACILITY MOST UTILIZED BY YOUR

    CLIENTELE? RANK THE FOLLOWING ACCORDING TO THE FREQUENCY OF

    USE, 1 BEING THE HIGHEST:

    1. Late Afternoon   4. Early Morning
    2. Evening   5. Mid-Morning
    3. Noon   6. Early Afternoon

24. RANK THE FOLLOWING DAYS ACCORDING TO THE FREQUENCY OF USE, 1

    BEING THE HIGHEST.

    1. Monday   4. Thursday   7. Sunday
    2. Wednesday   5. Saturday
    3. Tuesday   6. Friday

FIGURE 1 (continued)

25. RANK THE FOLLOWING MONTHS ACCORDING TO THE FREQUENCY OF USE, 1 BEING THE HIGHEST.

1. January	4. April	7. September	10. July
2. February	5. May	8. June	11. December
3. March	6. October	9. November	12. August

26. DOES YOUR FACILITY OFFER OR REQUIRE THAT AN INDIVIDUAL HEALTH ASSESSMENT PROFILE BE DEVELOPED ON EACH MEMBER?

Yes   64.1%   No   35.9%

27. DOES YOUR FACILITY OFFER ANY OF THE FOLLOWING SELF-HELP PROGRAMS?

1. Weight Reduction	87.2%
2. Alcohol Rehabilitation	12.8%
3. Drug Abuse	10.3%

Other: Women's Support Groups, Color Analysis, Wardrobe, Legal Counseling, Employment Seminars, Divorce Adjustment, Assertiveness Training, Sport Injury Prevention and Rehabilitation.

28. DO YOU OFFER ANY ONGOING EDUCATION IN THE FOLLOWING HEALTH RELATED AREAS?

Listed In Order Of Highest Reported Frequency:

Nutrition, Stress Management, CPR, Heart Attack Risk Reduction, Aquatic Therapy, Physical Therapy, Prenatal Exercises, Heimlich Maneuver, Post Partum Depression, Breast Self-Exam, Natural Childbirth, Parenting, Post Mastectomy, Dental Disease Prevention.

29. DOES YOUR FACILITY OFFER ANY OF THE FOLLOWING ADDITIONAL SERVICES?

Listed In Order Of Highest Reported Frequency:

Aerobics, Conditioning, Swimming, Dance, Diet, Racquetball, Hypertension, Cardiac Rehabilitation, Diabetes Control, Tennis, Home Management, Emergency Medicine, Screening, Cancer Risk Reduction, Sports Medicine, Knee-Shoulder-Back Rehabilitation Therapy.

30. IN THIS YEAR OF THE OLYMPICS, DOES YOUR FACILITY HAVE ANY SPECIAL PROMOTIONAL PLANS GEARED TOWARD THIS EVENT?

No	Yes	No Response
71.1%	26.3%	2.6%

Examples Include: Community Events, Mailers, Olympic Torch Run Support, Indoor Olympics, Medals and Trophies (Men and Women), Fund Raising.

FIGURE 1 (continued)

31. DOES YOUR FACILITY HAVE A STRUCTURED MARKETING PLAN?

Yes	No	No Response
82.1%	15.4%	3.0%

32. HOW DID YOU CHOOSE YOUR PARTICULAR LOCATION?

Close to Target Population	76.9%
Area of Consumer Demand	76.9%
Easy Access	64.1%
High Visibility	61.5%
Real Estate Considerations	46.2%
Selected by Corporate Headquarters	38.5%

33. DO YOU DIRECT ANY OF YOUR PROMOTIONAL ACTIVITIES TO A

SPECIFIC TARGET POPULATION?

Yes	No	No Response
89.2%	8.1%	2.7%

Examples Include: Prospectus of Population Growth, Based on
Member Profile, Immediate Area, 25-40 Year Old Upwardly
Mobile Men and Women, Women 20-41 Years, Working Women With
Young Children, Cardiac Patients, Physicians, Clergy, 3-5
Mile Radius, Home Owners.

34. IN WHICH OF THE FOLLOWING TYPES OF PROMOTION DOES YOUR

FACILITY PARTICIPATE?

Word-Of-Mouth	97.0%	Newspaper, Radio	51.5%
Mail Out	87.9%	Television	42.4%
Professional Referral	81.8%	Magazine	36.4%
Telephone	57.6%	Billboard	12.1%

Other: Telemarketing, Newsletter, Posters, Yellow Pages,
Brochures, Busbacks, Hand-Delivered Magazines.

35. WHICH OF THE ABOVE DOES YOUR FACILITY CONSIDER TO BE YOUR

MOST EFFECTIVE MARKETING TECHNIQUE?

Word of Mouth	97%
Direct Mailers	88%
Newspaper	52%
Professional Referrals, Public Service Announcements, Brochures	5%

Radio, Television, Telephone, Location
    To Hospital, Professional Staff,
    Magazines, Billboards, Weekly Guide,
    Yellow Pages
	5%

FIGURE 1 (continued)

CORPORATE FITNESS/WELLNESS ANALYSIS

To supplement the findings from the fitness center questionnaires, it was determined that on-site interviews with a varied group of employers would be valuable. The purpose of these interviews was to determine the state of the art among Dallas employers regarding support for and promotion of employee fitness/wellness programs. A group of 20 companies was independently selected for confidential interviews. Those interviewed included: XEROX; IBM; Control Data; Presbyterian Hospital; Baylor Medical Center; Dallas Independent School District; Adena Exploration; Texas Instruments Incorporated; Eagle Oil & Gas Co.; Frito-Lay; Eppler, Guerin & Turner—Stock Brokers; City of Dallas; Livingwell —Consultant Services; Dallas Police Department; Dorchester Gas; Fina Oil; L.W.F.W.—Marketing/Management Services; American Airlines; National Chemsearch; and Prudential Insurance of America. This group represented the gamut of small to large and public to private types of organizations. For each interview, the corporate manager of the fitness program or the benefits manager was contacted. A common list of interview questions was reviewed with each manager. Additionally, each manager was encouraged to share informally any significant remarks concerning their organization's participation in the employee fitness/wellness movement. Specifically, the managers were asked to address the following issues:

1. Does your company sponsor/hold fitness programs on site?
2. Do many of your employers hold memberships in community/commercially sponsored fitness clubs?
3. Do you reimburse your employees for the costs associated with participating in a fitness program?
4. Do you offer ongoing educational wellness programs on site (i.e., stress management or nutrition counseling, etc.)?
5. Do you allow flextime working hours for employees to participate in fitness programs?
6. Is prescreening or a health assessment conducted on your employees?
7. Is your fitness program membership considered part of your company's benefit package?
8. Do you keep and record data on employee fitness outcomes

that may be quantified for cost effectiveness program measurements?

9. Do you sponsor/offer recreational activities for employees and their families?
10. What is your top management's attitude toward and involvement in employee fitness programs?

The information obtained in the corporate interviews revealed that a wide range of employer sponsored wellness activities exists in Dallas. Responses regarding the specifics of corporate involvement covered the continuum of "It's up to the individual" to "Not sure what we do" to "We need to think about that" to highly detailed descriptions of company sponsored activities. The information generated from the interviews was summarized as follows:

—Programs were primarily initiated as a result of top level executive support of and involvement in fitness and health promotion activities or in an attempt to contain the costs associated with: medical care benefits, reduce setbacks from previous illnesses, increase morale measures, reduce absenteeism, reduce premature deaths, enhance recruitment/retention programs, increase productivity, improve self-image, and reduce employee turnover. Interviewees believed that fitness/wellness programs did/would improve each of the above employer concerns.

—On-site comprehensive fitness/wellness programs were offered by eight of the companies. Three of these also sponsored ongoing recreational activities for family members. A combination of company operated and contract managed fitness programs were used at the on-site locations. Five subsidized off-site fitness memberships and the remainder sponsored no organized programs and left it up to the individual employee.

—Employers offering on-site programs reported positive feedback and worker satisfaction with their facilities. Several noted that employees perceived that employer sponsored programs were of a higher quality than those available in community settings and promoted a "My Employer Cares About Me" attitude. These programs also experienced greater management leadership and support and had the highest company-wide employee involvement.

—Data to quantify or verify the cost benefits of corporate programs were not currently kept by any company even though plans for this were underway at four corporations.

—Little or no data is currently maintained to document changes in insurance premiums paid since initiating health promotion activities. Several managers reported that Blue Cross, Aetna, and Prudential have allowed some reduced premiums for participation in fitness programs.

—Employer financial support for fitness program participation varies. Fifty percent of those interviewed subsidized from 30% to 100% of a fitness program membership with employee contributions ranging from $0 to $150 annually. Two companies include this activity in their corporate benefits package.

—Flextime hours or staggered shifts for fitness participation were offered by four companies. Those with on-site facilities offer extended hours of operation and provide towel and locker room facilities.

—Some form of initial health profile screening was used by companies who sponsored programs. These ranged from highly detailed, medically oriented individual assessments to basic "lifestyle" questionnaires.

—Screenings were helpful in detecting cardiovascular, diabetic, and high blood pressure problems. The customized individual assessments also provided baseline data against which an employee's health performance could be measured. Aerobic, stress, and blood work testing were common screenings. None offered diagnostic screenings but several conducted breast cancer detection training. Weight reduction and smoking and alcohol succession programs were popular.

—Activities for computerizing individual fitness data were being initiated by three companies. In all cases, health/fitness data profiles were regarded as confidential material.

—Peer pressure was viewed as the strongest catalyst to achieve greater company-wide fitness participation but no reports of ostracism of nonparticipants were reported.

Based on the information shared in the corporate interviews, it can be stated that Dallas employers recognize that promoting employee fitness/wellness is a growing and multi-beneficial organizational activity. To date, corporate support for these programs is in varying stages of development whether sponsoring on-site or community-based programs. However, many Dallas employers are actively engaged in investigating the "Why, Where, What, and How To's" of employee fitness/health promotion programs as they affect all categories of their employees' corporate and personal WELL-NESS status.

CONCLUSION

Fitness/Wellness is both BIG BUSINESS and GOOD BUSI-NESS in Dallas County! Both the high response rate to the Fitness Center Questionnaire and the genuine interest expressed by employers substantiate this statement. Although it is recognized that Dallas is a young, growing, and progressive city, the findings in this study indicate that the Fitness/Wellness movement in Dallas presents entrepreneurial marketing opportunities for both business and health delivery managers.

Corporations are expressing much interest in discovering cost-effective approaches for limiting the escalating dollars they find themselves spending for health care benefits. As a result, they recognize that WELL employees are less costly and more productive. Another positive outcome of management's interest in promoting health and reducing illness-care costs may be the recognition of the intangible rewards that healthy people generate for the organization (creativity, team spirit, enthusiasm, etc.). Also, employees and retirees acknowledge that their whole family may benefit from participation in wellness-directed activities. This phenomenon results in even greater cost savings for both the employer and the employee as discussions of higher insurance premium co-payments become commonplace.

To conclude, we found that the wellness/fitness movement is rapidly spreading across Dallas County. We advise that any corporation or individual seeking to establish a fitness regimen (simple or sophisticated) research, visit, and evaluate the variety of programs currently available. Potential corporate fitness directors are encouraged to become familiar with their peers in this growing industry and to contact the Association for Fitness in Business. Opportunities for participants, sponsors, and marketers are many. The exciting growth of this movement clearly indicates that the new marriage between business organizations and health-care delivery visionaries has only just begun!

RECOMMENDATIONS FOR PROGRAM MANAGERS

To assist a fitness/wellness program manager (whether free-standing or corporate-based) with maximizing their marketing effectiveness while promoting enhanced organizational participant evaluations, the following ideas/activities are offered for consideration:

— Capitalize on "The Year of the Olympics" by providing video-tapes of past Olympic events to promote enthusiasm for personal/individual wellness. Award T-shirts with center/1984 Olympic logo to individual achievers.
— Market hospital-based center services to in-house staff and physicians. Educate community professionals about the scope of your services in order to gain a referral base. Host tours and free work-out sessions for selected target markets.
— Institute a "buddy-system" rehabilitation incentive program. Allow a complimentary visit for the "helper" of the disabled member.
— Promote special fees/activities to senior citizen organizations. Design competitive events between different senior groups.
— Offer continuing education for in-house employees with a percentage of reimbursement based on satisfactory course completion.
— Make TV monitors available for daytime soap opera watching for lunch hour exercise enthusiasts.
— Offer a referral incentive fee to program members.
— Award complimentary visits to volunteers who transport and assist disabled children or retired citizens.
— Secure public service radio spots to promote special events/competitive offerings.
— Solicit complimentary wearing apparel and personalized awards gadgets from retailers to use at special events.
— Include a description of the program's services and facilities in the parent organization's general recruiting brochures.
— Transmit activities or schedule classes for clients via cable programming.
— Emphasize and train employees to promote genuine caring and courteous behavior when conducting all activities or classes.
— Design wellness/fitness programs tailored to special events

than can be marketed to community and neighboring corporate clients.

—Host open houses for "corporate-nite" to managers, employees, and family members so they may visit and become familiar with your program.

—Poll current membership to self-assess present level of services and request recommendations.

—Target Saturday or after-school special events for children of members or develop unique programs for juveniles or teen-age organizations.

—Employee incentives are necessary to increase and retain active participation. The employee must have ample knowledge about the program's content and cost. Management may wish to consider some form of flextime, extended hours, or staggered shifts so employees may more conveniently utilize facilities.

—Provide free T-shirts, shorts, or socks with the company logo to increase the sense of team spirit and camaraderie.

—Create a positive attitude about absenteeism by doing away with sick days and substituting credit in the form of "well days". A positive "wellness" company attitude creates an atmosphere favoring rewarding presence on the job. An accrual schedule of days off, pay, or subsidization of the membership fee for "well days" might be effective.

—Keep members aware of improvements on their individual health profile. Acknowledging concrete improvements can serve as positive psychological reinforcement to increase participation and retention. (Give "gold stars"—i.e., cash, time off—for outstanding personal fitness achievements.)

—Publicize positive WELLNESS outcomes in corporate newsletters.

REFERENCES

Action, Journal of Association for Fitness in Business, March/April, 1984.

Benson, Jr., Edward M., "Business Is Advised To Be a Partner with Health Industry in Curbing Costs," *FAH Review*, January/February, 1984.

Cohen, Irving J., "Fit Employees Fatten the Bottom Line," *Inc.*, February, 1982.

Feinstein, Barbara and Brown, Edwin, *The New Partnership*, Schenkman Publishing Company, Inc., Cambridge, Massachusetts, 1982.

Kaufman, Jane G., "State of the Art: Physical Fitness in Corporations," *Employee Services Management*, February, 1983.

Kotz, H.J. and Fielding, J.G., eds., "Health Education and Promotion, Agenda for the Eighties," Summary report of an insurance industry conference on health education and promotion, Atlanta, Georgia, March 16-18, 1980.

Levine, A., "American Business Is Bullish on Wellness," *Medical World News*, March 29, 1982.

Novelli, William D., "Marketing: How Is It Working?", Guest Editorial in the *Journal of Health Care Marketing*, Fall, 1983.

Parkinson, Rebecca S. and Associates, *Managing Health Promotion in the Workplace*, Mayfield Publishing Company, Palo Alto, California, 1982.

Pelletier, Kenneth R., "Employee Health," *Medical Self-Care*, Spring, 1984.

Pelletier, Kenneth R., *Healthy People in Unhealthy Places: Stress and Fitness at Work*, Delacorte Press, 1984.

Richards, Glenn, "Business Examines Hospitals," *Hospitals*, January, 1984.

Windsor, R.A., Baranowski, T., Clark N., and G. Cutter, *Evaluation of Health Promotion and Educational Programs*, Palo Alto, California: Mayfield Publishing Company, 1984.

A Market Research Analysis of an Occupational Health Services Program

Dennis R. McDermott

INTRODUCTION

Based on increased competition in the hospital and health care services marketplace, a gradual evolution from a seller's market to a buyer's market has taken place. Traditionally, hospitals have viewed their marketing mission as being twofold, namely first, to recruit and maintain a competent staff of physicians and nurses, and second, to ensure patients receive satisfaction regarding their care and treatment. While these two areas will obviously remain significant for hospitals successfully marketing health care services environmental factors are requiring a broadening and redefining of market targets for future success. An example of this market redefinition and segmentation is described by the following illustration of a market research study designed to investigate the feasibility of an Occupational Health Services Program, as defined by the following OHSP Concept Statement:

The Occupational Health Services Program would consist of health care services provided by an area hospital to employees through their employer on a contractual basis. Depending on the specific service the care may be given either at the employer's location, at the hospital, or at a satellite facility near the employer operated by the hospital. These health care services would include first, treatment of on-the-job illnesses or injuries; second, pre-placement and periodic physical exams and screening tests; and third, health maintenance or illness pre-

Dennis R. McDermott, PhD, is Associate Professor of Marketing, School of Business, Virginia Commonwealth University, 1015 Floyd Avenue, Richmond, Virginia 23284.

91

vention programs. This Occupational Health Services Program is designed to address the state of your employees' health on a continual basis, and where practical, allow for economies of scale. As a result, benefits could be realized by employers due to increased employee productivity and reduced health care costs.

METHODOLOGY

In order to generate data to test the feasibility of the OHSP and to prioritize employer market targets, a telephone survey was conducted of 66 major employers located within approximately a 10 mile radius of the hospital sponsoring the study. Respondent job titles varied by employer, but generally the person interviewed was the personnel manager or employee benefits manager. The general categories of employers and the number in each who were interviewed along with the total numbers of employees represented are as follows:

1. Government/Education (10-26,000)
2. Manufacturers with more than 1,000 employees (7-22,000)
3. Service firms with more than 1,000 employees (14-24,000)
4. Manufacturers with from 300 to 1,000 employees (9-5,500)
5. Service firms with from 300 to 1,000 employees (26-12,000)

The questionnaire used in the study consisted of four areas, including determining:

1. The extent of medical care employers are providing employees on-premise and their perceived satisfaction regarding quality and cost;
2. The employers' perceived expected benefits, i.e., significant, moderate, or no benefits on hearing the OHSP Concept Statement;
3. The employer's perceptions of how significant the benefits would be regarding the three components of the OHSP, namely first, treating on-the-job illnesses or injuries; second, giving physical exams and screening tests; and third, providing health maintenance or illness prevention programs;
4. The employers' preferred hospital, if one exists, and the relative preference ratings of three specified hospitals.

STUDY RESULTS

The study results are presented in the same sequence as the four questionnaire areas just indicated. Regarding on-premise medical care, as might be expected, those employers that employ a staff of full-time physicians and nurses are all of the manufacturers with more than 1,000 employees. Most require a pre-placement physical exam given by this medical staff, but generally offer continual physical exams to only the high-level employees. All indicated a moderate to high degree of satisfaction with the quality and cost-effectiveness of having their own medical staff on-premise. However, these employers' concern regarding overall health care costs is evidenced by most of them offering a Health Maintenance Organization alternative to employees instead of their health insurance policy. Only two of the 14 service firms with more than 1,000 employees employ medical personnel, generally for the purpose of giving pre-placement physical exams. Four of the nine manufacturing firms employing from 300 to 1,000 employees have a medical staff, but these are generally limited to a full-time nurse and in two cases a part-time physician. Just two of the 26 service firms employing from 300 to 1,000 employees have medical personnel who treat injuries, illnesses, and give pre-placement physicals.

OHSP CONCEPT STATEMENT PERCEPTIONS

Table 1 summarizes, by employer category, their perceptions of how significant the benefits of the OHSP Concept Statement would be to their employers and employees.

Of significance is the fact that of the 58 respondents who had a distinct perception of the OHSP Concept Statement, some 38 or 66 percent perceived moderate or significant benefits. The common expressed reason for a "don't know" response was that while the OHSP Concept Statement sounded appealing, they would need more specific information on which to base their perception. Of additional interest is the relative negative perceptions of manufacturers, both large and moderate in size, who, as expressed earlier, are far more likely to have medical employees than the government, educational, or service firms, who indicated a generally favorable set of perceptions. If the manufacturers are excluded from Table 1, of the 42 employers who gave an opinion of the perceived benefits, 32 or 76 percent indicated moderate or significant benefits. Of the 16

	Significant	Moderate	No Benefits	Don't Know
Government/Education	3	3	1	1
Manufacturing > 1,000		3	4	
Services > 1,000	1	7	5	1
Manufacturing: 300 to 1,000	1	2	5	1
Services: 300 to 1,000	5	13	5	3
Totals	10	28	20	8

TABLE 1. Summary of Employer Perceptions of OSHP Concept Statement Benefits

employers who currently offer an HMO alternative to employees, all but one expressed a perception to the OHSP Concept Statement, with 10 or 67 percent indicating they perceived moderate or significant benefits.

The 20 respondents who perceived no benefits from the OHSP Concept Statement were not asked any additional questions. The remaining 46, however, were asked their perceptions regarding each of the three components of the OHSP Concept Statement. Table 2 indicates that of those expressing an opinion, 26 out of 37 respondents, or 70 percent, perceive moderate or significant benefits regarding the OHSP approach to treating on-the-job illnesses or injuries. It should be pointed out that when this question was asked, it was indicated to each respondent that if the illness or injury required a trip to the hospital, the employee would not go through the emergency room procedure but rather to a separate area allowing for faster treatment. In addition, the usage of mobile or satellite facilities could be feasible for such illness or injury cases.

Table 3 points out the respondents' perceptions of benefits if the OHSP provided physical exams or screening tests at a 25 percent cost savings. Of those giving an opinion, 33 out of 40, or 83 percent, perceive the benefits to be moderate or significant. Of the seven who perceive no benefits, six indicated they don't currently give physical exams so no savings would be realized. From comments given by respondents, two generalizations can be made regarding physical exams. First, those employers who have employees requiring pre-placement and annual physicals, e.g., policemen, firemen, bus and truck drivers, are very concerned about the high cost of these exams and are constantly looking for alternatives. Second, with the exception of the specific jobs mentioned above, and in some cases upper-level management positions, a preplacement physical exam is the only one given to employees, which is usually arranged and paid for by the employee. While most employers feel an annual or biannual physical exam for all employees is an excellent policy to boost employee productivity, and also generates long-run cost-savings by preventing more costly employee health problems in the future, very few are following through with a formalized or structured employee physical exam procedure.

Table 4 indicates the employers' perceptions of the benefits re-

	Significant	Moderate	No Benefits	Don't Know
Government/Education	4	1	2	3
Manufacturing: > 1,000	1	2		
Services: > 1,000	2	3	1	2
Manufacturing: 300 to 1,000	2	1	1	
Services: 200 to 1,000	2	8	7	4
Totals	11	15	11	9

TABLE 2. EMPLOYER PERCEPTIONS OF BENEFITS FROM OHSP APPROACH TO TREATING ON-THE-JOB ILLNESSES OR INJURIES

	Significant	Moderate	No Benefits	Don't Know
Government/Education	2	3		4
Manufacturing: > 1,000	1	2		
Services: > 1,000	2	6		1
Manufacturing: 300 to 1,000		2	1	1
Services: 300 to 1,000	6	9	6	—
Totals	11	22	7	6

TABLE 3. EMPLOYER PERCEPTIONS OF BENEFITS FROM OHSP COST SAVINGS OF 25 PERCENT REGARDING PHYSICAL EXAMS OR SCREENING TESTS

	Significant	Moderate	No Benefits	Don't Know
Government/Education	5	3		1
Manufacturing: > 1,000	2	1		
Services: > 1,000	7	2		
Manufacturing: 300 to 1,000	2	1	1	
Services: 300 to 1,000	6	12	1	2
Totals	22	19	2	3

TABLE 4: EMPLOYER PERCEPTIONS OF BENEFITS FROM OHSP HEALTH MAINTENANCE PROGRAMS

garding health maintenance programs provided by the OHSP, which were defined to include such areas as physical fitness, nutrition, smoking, alcohol, drugs, anxiety and stress. As the data point out, of those expressing an opinion, 41 out of 43, or 95 percent of the respondents, perceive the benefits to be moderate or significant.

HOSPITAL PREFERENCES

When the 46 employers were asked if there was a particular hospital they would prefer if their employer was to enter into a contractual arrangement for occupational health care services, only 11 mentioned a specific hospital. When asked why they preferred that hospital, proximity of location was the reason in every case. In addition, preference ratings were obtained on a high, moderate, or low scale, from the employers for three specified hospitals. Only about one-half of those interviewed gave a response other than "don't know." The differences in the relative perceptions regarding their preferences for a specified hospital was again mostly highly correlated with that hospital's location. Some additional reasons given as justification for a high preference included quality of care, experience, and having certain specialized programs such as psychiatry, while reasons for a low preference included inconsistent billing procedures and long delays in the emergency room.

SUMMARY

Based on a market research study conducted by interviewing 66 personnel and employee benefits managers of major employers, defined as having more than 300 employees, some generalizations or conclusions can be made regarding the concept of an Occupational Health Services Program, whereby a hospital markets health care services directly to employers on a contractual basis. The concern that employers have regarding health care costs is evidenced by 66 percent of the employers perceiving either moderate or significant benefits, with government, educational, and service firms being more likely to react favorably to the OHSP Concept Statement. The fact that some employers interviewed offer an HMO alternative did not alter their perceptions of the OHSP benefits. When the subsample who perceived either moderate or significant benefits regarding the OHSP, i.e., 66 percent of the total sample of employers, was interviewed further regarding specific components of the OHSP, the reactions tended to become more favorable. First, 70 percent of the respondents perceive moderate or significant benefits regarding the OHSP approach to treating on-the-job illnesses or injuries. Second, 83 percent perceive the benefits of the OHSP giving physical exams and screening test at a 25 percent cost savings to be moderate or significant. Third, 95 percent perceive moderate or significant benefits regarding the OHSP offering health maintenance or illness prevention programs. Relatively few of the respondents indicated a specific hospital that would be preferred if a contractual health care program was set up, and those who indicated a preference did so due to the proximity of the hospital.

SECTION THREE:
EMPHASIS ON PREPAID
HEALTH PLANS:
HMOs, PPOs, AND INSURANCE

A tremendous interest has materialized in the aspect of contracting during the last couple of years. We have entered the decade of abbreviations as we explore HMOs, PPOs, IPAs, etc. The oldest form of contracting has been the prepaid mode of delivery and insurance coverage. As providers and third-party payers seek modes which provide some form of consistent demand for their services (through a formal contract) and are less costly to the consumer, the ambulatory care section of the industry will continue to experiment with different forms of prepaid plans and services.

This section explores some basic marketing implications of these new ambulatory care areas by examining HMOs, PPOs, and Insurance. Since some HMOs have been in existence for many years we can learn a considerable amount from these organizations. There are also a considerable amount of literary resources on how to market HMOs and prepaid health plans. Gradually, this literature is expanding for contracting ambulatory care services such as group practices, urgent care centers, and wellness and stress management programs.

The prepaid and contracting format of ambulatory care is just "tipping the iceberg" for its potential growth. These articles should provide some good strategy examples in marketing HMOs, PPOs, Prepaid Plans, and Insurance.

WJW

99

The Selling of an HMO:
A Field Test of the Questionnaire
as Marketing Tool

David G. Schmeling
Winifred H. Schmeling

INTRODUCTION

Marketing new Health Maintenance Organizations (HMOs) is essential for success yet can be incredibly difficult. The HMO concept can be vague, abstract and hard to grasp. Cost comparisons can be complex and benefit packages notoriously hard to compare considering co-insurance, deductibles, co-payments, and exclusions. The enrollment choice frequently involves a change in providers of care.

Timing too is critical, when penetration of particular employee groups must be carefully sized to the resources available. Additionally, marketing must target the group(s) which will provide a sound actuarial base for the plan. The benefit package must be assembled and priced to minimize adverse selection.

Ironically, many of these marketing decisions hinge on the very information least likely to be available—demographic and psychographic data on target populations. For HMOs to succeed, awareness must be high, a situation all too often absent in many communities today where fledgling HMOs are struggling for survival.

This is a case study of one HMO's use of the questionnaire as a marketing tool for both gathering data and enhancing community awareness.

Dave Schmeling, PhD, is the Administrator of Florida's Children's Mental Health Programs, a consultant on media and marketing designs and frequent contributor to mental health and communication publications.

Winnie Schmeling, RN, PhD, is Executive Vice President of MGT of America, Inc., a Tallahassee-based national management consulting firm and Vice-Chairman of the Board of Capital Health Plan, Inc. The Schmelings are husband and wife.

BACKGROUND

The sole HMO in the community, Capital Health Plan (CHP), serves Tallahassee, Florida a non-industrial metropolitan area of 175,000, the economic base for which is state government and two universities.

Feasibility studies for CHP began in 1979 under the Federal HMO grant and loan program. There had been some interest in HMO development in the community earlier, but it drew heavy fire from the medical and hospital community. Over time, resistance to the HMO dissipated owing in part to a family practice residency program in the community which caused a dramatic increase in and redistribution of primary care physicians. This somewhat neutralized the potency of specialists as well as generated providers willing to work in a staff model HMO.

At the same time, political pressures were growing at the state level for lower cost health care alternatives. The health plan for state employees had been maintained at artificially low prices by a trust fund which was running low. The legislature decided to cut the benefits and raise deductibles as well as premiums. This made the HMO package price-competitive and the benefit package more attractive.

The success of the plan depended on essentially a single employer, state government. In addition to segmenting the market by the usual variables, the marketing was segmented by the various state departments. The marketing plan had to be carefully timed since enrollment would need to be controlled. The initial strategy also had to anticipate that potential enrollees knew little or nothing about HMOs, and CHP knew little or nothing about them. For this reason it was decided to incorporate in the marketing approach a device which would convey information to the potential enrollee, and in return yield critical marketing information for the HMO. The questionnaire was this vehicle.

This marketing activity was undertaken in conjunction with a field experimental study (Schmeling, 1981) which sought to provide a rare public test of the effectiveness of the questionnaire as a marketing device.

THE QUESTIONNAIRE

The use of questionnaires as data gathering devices is commonplace. The "Questionnaire Effect"—the information transmitting property of the instrument—was recognized as long ago as 1939 (Schanck & Goodman, 1939), but its effectiveness as information transmitter has only recently enjoyed scientific interest.

The questionnaire, as marketing device, has seen dramatic growth over the past few years. Its use by the Moral Majority, the Heritage Foundation, the National Foundation for Cancer Research and various political groups has mushroomed. The questionnaire as a tool for fund-raising is particularly popular.

Historically, studies of the effects of questionnaires have dealt with: 1) attitudes 2) diagnostic assessments such as personality adjustment or I.Q. scores and 3) information transfer.

When taken as a whole, the literature with respect to attitudes, diagnostic situations and information transfer is equivocal. When information-transfer studies are examined apart from the total body of literature, however, coherent patterns emerge which strongly suggest that the questionnaire enhances issue salience and stimulates information seeking, especially when the information has instrumental utility or usefulness.

Interest in a topic is correlated with exposure. Continued or increased exposure may be induced by stimulated interest (Berelson, Lazarsfeld & McPhee, 1954; Lazarsfeld, Berelson & Gaudet 1948; Weiss, 1969) producing an "exposure-knowledge spiral" (Atkin, Galloway & Nayman, 1976). Questionnaires may, through a complex series of relationships, make subjects aware of and seek information on both salient and non-salient issues alike (Crespi, 1948; Jahoda, Deutsch & Cook, 1951; Nosanchuk & Marchak, 1969).

Factors accounting for issue salience—the relative priority an individual assigns to a topic—are diverse: press coverage, personal interest; even occupation or education may predict what is important and on which topics additional information will be sought.

The effect of the questionnaire in enhancing issue salience and subsequent information-seeking seems to be a function of four main factors: the defenses down phenomenon, the demand effect of the experimenter, commitment and importance conferral. The defenses down effect is the open, cooperative unsuspecting mind-set on the part of the respondent stemming from one's belief that the sponsor of the questionnaire has nothing to gain from her or him personally (Hovland, Janis & Kelley, 1953). The demand effect is the tendency of subjects to respond privately to the expectations of the experimenter (Crespi, 1948; Orne, 1962; Rosenthal, 1976). Commitment may occur by virtue of the respondent "publicly" asserting one's views. The respondent may feel important by virtue of being selected to present his or her views.

THE STUDY

To test the effectiveness of the questionnaire in enhancing issue salience, a design was employed which compared the questionnaire with a conventional medium in widespread use, the brochure.

The brochure was selected as the control condition because it does not enjoy the defenses down, demand effect, committing, or importance conferral properties of the questionnaire. It was expected that the questionnaire would enhance issue saliency and information seeking more than a brochure on the same topic.

Methodology

In a controlled case study using a field experimental design three conditions, questionnaire alone, brochure alone, and questionnaire and brochure in combination, were mailed with a business reply card to a random sample of 3,000 non-duplicated State of Florida career service (civil service) and university employees living in Leon County (Tallahassee) Florida. Differential rates of return of business reply cards requesting additional information on CHP reflected the efficacy of each condition in heightening issue salience and prompting information seeking. A cover letter from CHP (Appendix A) accompanied each treatment. Those individuals assigned to the brochure-only treatment who returned a business reply card were mailed the questionnaire upon receipt of the reply card. The time allowed for subjects to respond to the mailing was five weeks.

The twenty-one item questionnaire (Appendix B) sought information about current health care, insurance practices, perceptions and respondent demographics. The return postage-paid questionnaire was designed to be folded and mailed independent of the business reply card to assure anonymity. Each questionnaire was unobtrusively color coded by a distinguishing mark to the margin to facilitate grouping by treatment. Care was exercised in the questionnaire preamble and question construction to minimize bias.

The brochure (Appendix C) was a professionally produced two-color eight-panel piece designed to increase recipient awareness of the HMO concept and of CHP.

In addition to soliciting name and address, the business reply card (Appendix D) measured health insurance, demographic characteristics and the recipients' perceived personal involvement in the issue.

Data Analysis

The chi square one sample test was used to determine whether the business reply card response rates from the three groups differed significantly from chance expectations. A comparison was performed on each possible combination of two variables and on the three treatments taken as a group. Demographic differences were analyzed by chi square. For all analyses the alpha level was .05.

RESULTS

The Questionnaire Effect

Table 1 presents the frequency of return of business reply card responses among the three treatment groups.

The results of a chi square one sample test performed on these data reveal no significance at the .05 level ($x^2 = 4.28$; df = 2; p .10). Likewise, the questionnaire in combination with the brochure was not demonstrated to be more potent than the brochure alone. Indeed, brochure-only subjects returned the business reply cards at a greater rate than did recipients of the combination.

TABLE 1

FREQUENCY OF RETURN OF BUSINESS REPLY CARDS

	Treatment Groups		
	Questionnaire	Questionnaire: Brochure (combination)	Brochure
Business Reply Card Responses (Dependent variable)	92	66	79

DISCUSSION

Several factors may have contributed to the outcome of this study. First, contrary to conventional research designs where differences among treatments are maximized, treatments in this study were similarly constructed to standardize the amount of information available to each group. While this was necessary to control the information variable, it diminished uniqueness of treatments. Had creative, persuasive advertising been employed in the design and wording of the questionnaire, the outcome may have been different. Standardizing the amount of information for each treatment likewise increased the bulk of the mailed materials to the "combination" group and resulted in duplicative material being included in the mailing to these individuals. Responses from this group may have been inhibited simply because subjects were unwilling to deal with so abundant a mailing.

A provocative further question suggests itself from this study. What would be the effect on subsequent information-seeking of a business reply card with questionnaire features alone? Such an approach is clearly superior from a cost standpoint, would likely elicit as many responses from already committed respondents as would any treatment employed here, and may be as effective in enhancing issue salience.

That significance was absent in this study in no way discredits the questionnaire's impact as reported in other investigations. In fact, in this study, the questionnaire acquitted itself rather well against the popular brochure, performing at least as well as the conventional medium and demonstrating the predicted directionality. Indeed the questionnaire is superior to conventional media because it generates needed data which permit descriptive analyses of populations and targeting of advertising campaigns to the "most likely prospects". It impacts issue salience for many recipients, whether respondents or not.

While this single marketing tool cannot be solely credited for CHP success, its contribution is undeniable. Capital Health Plan has exceeded by more than 50 percent its projected 8-10 percent penetration rates, and today is an affiliate of a major insurer, has negotiated favorable hospital and referral contracts, enjoys low drop-out rates and is generally regarded as one of the country's most successful HMOs.

REFERENCES

Atkin, C.K., Galloway, J. & Nayman, O.B. News media exposure: Political knowledge and campaign interest. *Journalism Quarterly*, 1976, *53*, 231-237.

Berelson, B., Lazarsfeld, P., & McPhee, W. *Voting*. Chicago: University of Chicago Press, 1954.

Crespi, L.P. The interview effect in polling. *Public Opinion Quarterly*, 1948, *12*, 99-111.

Hovland, C.I., Janis I.L., & Kelley, H.H. *Communication and Persuasion*. New Haven: Yale University Press, 1953.

Jahoda, M., Deutsch, M., & Cook, S.W. *Research Methods in Social Relations*. New York: Dryden Press, 1951.

Lazarsfeld, P.I., Berelson, B., & Gaudet, H. *The People's Choice*. New York: Columbia University Press, 1968.

Nosanchuk, T.A. & Marchak, M.P. Pretest Sensitization and Attitude Change, *Public Opinion Quarterly*, 1969, *33*, 107-111.

Orne, M.T. On the social psychology of the psychological experiment with particular reference to demand characteristics and their implication. *American Psychologist*, 1962, *17*, 776-783.

Rosenthal, R. *Experimenter Effects in Behavioral Research*. New York: Irvington Publishers, Inc. 1976.

Schanck, R.L. & Goodman, C. Reactions to propaganda on both sides of a controversial issue. *Public Opinion Quarterly*, 1939, *3*, 107-112.

Schmeling, D.G. The Questionnaire Effect: Information Transmitting Properties of Data Gathering Instruments. Unpublished Ph.D. Dissertation, Florida State University, June, 1981.

Weiss, W. Effects of the Mass Media of Communication. In G. Lindzey and E. Aronson (eds.) *The Handbook of Social Psychology*, (Vol. 5) Reading, Massachusetts: Addison-Wesley, 1969, 77-195.

APPENDIX A

CAPITAL GROUP HEALTH SERVICES OF FLORIDA, INC.   (904) 877-7162

A Developing Health Maintenance Organization

November 10, 1980

Dear "Neighbor":

As a State employee, you have the option of participating in a range of fringe benefit programs. Health insurance is a major feature of your fringe benefit package. Most State workers are currently enrolled in the State of Florida Group Health Insurance Program, and many have supplemented this coverage with additional policies at their own expense. There is a different type of health care program, an improved alternative to traditional health insurance, now being developed by your neighbors. We'd like to tell you about it.

Capital Group Health Services of Florida, Inc. is a private, non-profit corporation organized by local community leaders concerned about the rising cost of health care and committed to doing something about it. The corporation which is governed by local representatives from private management, State government, medicine, the academic community, labor, and consumer groups, is developing a health maintenance organization to serve this area. HMOs are health care delivery organizations which provide a comprehensive range of health services for a fixed, prepaid fee. When this HMO is operational, it will be included as a part of the State's health benefits program, and all full time employees and their families will be offered the option of HMO membership as an alternative to traditional insurance coverage.

As you may know, Governor Graham and his administration support policies which encourage the development of HMOs in Florida and want to see one established in Tallahassee. Support for HMOs stems from the comprehensiveness of the services they provide and their cost effectiveness. In many areas of the country, HMOs are able to reduce their members' total health care expenditures by 10 to 40 percent over those of conventional modes of insurance.

The number of HMOs has grown rapidly in recent years, and State employees have responded very favorably to the option of HMO membership in many areas of the country. The enclosed materials are intended to help us accurately determine whether a similar level of interest exists in this area. If you are interested, we would welcome your input and involvement in our program's development. We want this HMO to meet your needs.

I know health care is important to you and your family. Please take a few minutes to review the enclosed materials and let us hear from you. Your cooperation and attention are greatly appreciated.

Sincerely,

John Hogan
John Hogan
Executive Director

Enc.

327 OFFICE PLAZA DRIVE   •   SUITE 203   •   TALLAHASSEE, FLORIDA 32301

APPENDIX B

State Employee Questionnaire

The Capital Health Plan, a private, non-profit health maintenance organization (HMO), is a new system of health care delivery being developed by local citizens in Tallahassee. For a fixed, prepaid fee, the Capital Health Plan will provide or arrange for all doctors' services, hospitalization, emergency care worldwide, laboratory, x-ray, and a wide range of other health services, primarily through its Health Center in Tallahassee. The HMO will be competitively priced, and the premiums will be paid for in the same way that your existing health insurance is financed. The Plan will practically eliminate the out-of-pocket expenses you may now be paying for deductibles and co-insurance because one monthly premium provides full coverage.

This survey is designed to gather information on your current costs and feelings about health care, to help in planning this HMO. The organizers of the Capital Health Plan want to insure that this HMO meets *your* health care needs. Please take a few minutes to complete this questionnaire and return it today. No postage is required. Your responses are strictly confidential. Thank you.

1. Do you currently participate in the State of Florida Group Health Insurance Program through payroll deduction?

☐ Yes (1)   ☐ No (2)

If Yes, do you have:

1a. ☐ Individual Coverage (1)   ☐ Family Coverage (2)

If No, do you have:

1d. ☐ Other Insurance (1)   ☐ Uninsured (2)

1b. If you carry family coverage, how many individuals other than yourself are covered?

☐ Spouse (1)   [ ] 1c. Number of Dependent Children

2. Have you supplemented your current health coverage with any of these additional health insurance policies offered to State employees?

2a. ☐ Gulf Life 20/20 (1)   2b. ☐ Gabor (2)   2c. ☐ Cancer Care (3)   2d. ☐ Other (4)   2e. ☐ No (5)

3. Have you used your health insurance in the past year?

☐ Yes (1)   ☐ No (2)

4. In your opinion, how adequate is your health insurance?

☐ Very Inadequate (1)   ☐ Somewhat Inadequate (2)   ☐ Average (3)   ☐ Somewhat Adequate (4)   ☐ Very Adequate (5)   ☐ Don't Know (99)

5. What, if anything, would you change about your current health insurance?

☐ No deductibles— complete payment (1)   ☐ Preventive and routine exams covered (2)   ☐ Vision and dental coverage (3)   ☐ Other (4)   ☐ No Change (98)   ☐ Don't Know (99)

6. Please estimate the total household out-of-pocket costs you paid for health services (doctors, hospitals, lab, x-ray, etc.) last year excluding what you paid for health insurance and dental bills?

☐ Under $100 (1)   ☐ $100-$499 (2)   ☐ $500-$999 (3)   ☐ $1,000-$1,499 (4)   ☐ Over $1,500 (5)

7. How do you feel this figure compares with the average person's health services bills?

☐ Very much lower (1)   ☐ Somewhat lower (2)   ☐ Average (3)   ☐ Somewhat higher (4)   ☐ Very much higher (5)

And now, some questions about HMOs:

8. Before today, how much did you know about Health Maintenance Organizations (HMOs)?

☐ Nothing (1)   ☐ Some Knowledge (2)   ☐ A Fair Knowledge (3)

9. HMO monthly premium costs are sometimes slightly higher than existing insurance premiums because deductibles and co-payments are virtually eliminated and coverage is more comprehensive. If membership in an HMO practically eliminated your out-of-pocket costs for health services, would you be willing to personally pay a slight additional monthly premium?

☐ Yes (1)   ☐ No (2)   ☐ Don't Know (99)

10. Do you have a personal or family physician?

☐ Yes (1)   ☐ No (2)

10a. **If Yes, Because the HMO contracts with a select group of highly qualified doctors, joining an HMO may mean switching from your current physician. Would such a switch prevent you from joining an HMO?**

☐ Yes (1)   ☐ No (2)   ☐ Not Sure (99)

(Over)

APPENDIX B (continued)

11. If an HMO were available in Tallahassee, would you consider joining?

☐   ☐   ☐   ☐
No   Would possibly   Would definitely   Would definitely
(1)   consider joining   consider joining   join
                 (2)   (3)   (4)

11a. If you would consider joining would you enroll for?

☐   ☐
Individual coverage Family coverage
(1)   (2)

11b. If family coverage, number of family members you would enroll in addition to yourself?

☐
Spouse   ┌──────────┐
(1)   └──────────┘
                 Number of Dependent Children
                 (2)

The following information is requested for statistical and actuarial purposes only:

12. Your age _____

13. Sex   ☐   ☐
               Male   Female
               (1)   (2)

14. Marital Status   ☐   ☐
                            Single   Married
                            (1)   (2)

15. Race   ☐   ☐   ☐   ☐
               Black   White   Hispanic   Other
               (1)   (2)   (3)   (4)

16. Education:

☐   ☐   ☐   ☐   ☐   ☐
Less than   H.S.   Some   BA/   Graduate   Graduate
High School   Degree   College   BS   Work   Degree
(1)   (2)   (3)   (4)   (5)   (6)

17. Family members living in your household in addition to yourself.

☐
Spouse   ┌──────────┐
(1)   └──────────┘
                 Number of Dependent Children
                 (2)

17a. Please circle the age of each child
1   2   3   4   5   6   7   8   9   10   11   12   13   14   15   16   17   18   19   20   21   22   23

18. Into which category does your total household income fall?

☐   ☐   ☐   ☐   ☐   ☐   ☐   ☐
less than $10,000- $15,000- $20,000- $25,000- $30,000- $40,000-   Over
$10,000 $14,999 $19,999 $24,999 $29,999 $39,999 $49,999 $50,000
(1)   (2)   (3)   (4)   (5)   (6)   (7)   (8)

19. How many years have you lived in Tallahassee? _____

20. For which department of State government do you work?

☐   ☐   ☐   ☐   ☐   ☐   ☐   ☐
FSU   FAMU   HRS   Dept. of   Dept. of   Dept. of   Dept. of   Other, describe
(1)   (2)   (3)   Trans-   Education   Motor Vehicles   Labor and   (8)
                           portation   (5)   and Highway   Employment   _____
                           (4)   Safety   Security   _____
                                                       (6)   (7)   _____

Please fold with the return address outside, tape and mail. Thank you.

‖‖‖

APPENDIX C

Capital Health Plan

A New Way to Promote Good Health is Coming to Tallahassee!

And You Should Know About It

For more information about
Capital Health Plan
write or call:

Capital Group Health Services of Florida, Inc.
327 Office Plaza Drive, Suite 203
Tallahassee, Florida 32301
Phone: (904) 877-7162

What is Capital Health Plan?

Capital Health Plan is a Health Maintenance Organization (**HMO**), currently being developed by Capital Group Health Services of Florida, Inc. An HMO is an organized health care system which delivers a wide range of health care services to individuals and families who voluntarily enroll and who pay a fixed monthly fee. This prepaid fee covers everything from routine physical examinations to complete hospitalization and treatment by a wide range of health care specialists.

☐ Capital Group Health Services of Florida, Inc., a private, non-profit corporation was created by local citizens who are concerned with the rising cost of health care and the need for an alternative system of health care delivery. The organization was formed to develop the HMO alternative for the residents of Leon, Gadsden, and Wakulla Counties.

Capital Health Plan will offer the following basic services to its members.*

- All physician services, including consultation and referral care
- Complete hospitalization
- Medically necessary emergency health services required anywhere in the world
- Short-term mental health services
- Medical treatment and referral for abuse of and addiction to alcohol and drugs
- Diagnostic laboratory, x-ray, and therapeutic radiologic services

- Home health services
- Preventive health care services, including:
  – periodic adult physical examinations,
  – children's eye and ear examinations,
  – well child care from birth,
  – vision care,
  – immunization,
  – family planning & health education.

*This brochure describes the essential features of **Capital Health Plan** and is not intended to be a full description of coverage. A complete description of coverage will be provided in the contract issued to all participants.

APPENDIX C (continued)

Capital Health Plan is not another form of health insurance.

☐ Traditional health insurance plans only provide payment for certain types of medical expenses in the event of illness. As a result, many people only seek medical attention on a sickness or crisis oriented basis.

Capital Health Plan will provide a full range of health care services with emphasis on early disease detection. Preventive medicine is the focus of an HMO. You don't have to be sick to benefit from your membership.

☐ Most insurance plans contain exclusions, deductibles, and co-insurance requirements, forcing members to pay substantial out-of-pocket costs for services.

Capital Health Plan will practically eliminate out-of-pocket expense by providing full coverage of all health care benefits for one monthly premium.

Because your health care is prepaid, you won't be charged for services you require. There are no medical bills or claim forms to worry about in an HMO.

☐ Health insurance plans are primarily *bill paying organizations*, leaving the subscriber responsible for locating and acquiring needed services.

Capital Health Plan not only will pay bills, but also will arrange for the delivery of health care. An HMO is primarily a *health service organization* responsible for the accessibility and quality of care delivered.

How will Capital Health Plan deliver services to its members?

As a Capital Health Plan member, most of the health care you will need will be available to you at the HMO's health center, which will be located in Tallahassee. The Center is currently being designed and will be a modern, well-equipped facility, including doctors' offices, laboratory, x-ray, and supportive services. Hospital care and specialized referral services will be arranged for you when needed at local facilities. Should you require emergency treatment while traveling away from home, Capital Health Plan will cover it.

Capital Health Plan members will select their own personal, primary care physician from among the members of the medical group. The physician selected by the enrollee will coordinate all the member's health care needs, including referrals to specialists and hospitalization when required. Physicians participating with Capital Health Plan will practice in a group setting which fosters an organized peer review/quality assurance program without sacrificing the personal physician/member relationship.

How much will Capital Health Plan cost?

The cost of membership in the Capital Health Plan will be competitive with the monthly premium of a comprehensive major medical program. If you are currently covered by an employer group insurance plan, your employer will pay the same monthly amount towards your Capital Health Plan membership as is paid for your existing insurance. If the Capital Health Plan premium is higher, the additional cost would be borne by you. As a developing health maintenance organization, our final cost figures are not yet available. However, studies have shown that an HMO member's total health care expenses can be lower than a health insurance subscriber's, even if the monthly HMO premium is higher. This occurs because of the HMO's broader coverage of services which minimizes a member's out-of-pocket expenses.

HMOs have a proven record of success for over 50 years.

Currently, there are over 225 HMOs in operation nationally, including 8 in Florida, providing services to more than 8 million people. An additional 225 plans are expected to become operational HMOs during this decade, including this one in Tallahassee.

☐ HMOs are receiving national recognition as a strategy for solving many of the problems which accompany the current delivery of health care in the U.S. The HMO concept is supported by such diverse groups as the U.S. Chamber of Commerce, the AFL-CIO, the Washington Business Group on Health, and the American Medical Association-sponsored National Commission on Medical Care Costs. Governor Graham has made HMO growth and development in Florida a priority health care concern of his administration.

Enrollment? The choice will be yours.

Membership in a health maintenance organization represents an alternative to your present insurance coverage. You may select the Capital Health Plan option or maintain your present coverage—whichever best meets your needs. Capital Group Health Services of Florida wants your choice to be an informed one, and encourages you to contact us and have input into the planning and development of this area's first health maintenance organization.

APPENDIX D

First Class
Permit No. 131
Tallahassee, FL

BUSINESS REPLY CARD

No postage necessary if mailed in the United States.
Postage will be paid by:

Capital Group Health Services
327 Office Plaza Rd.
Suite 203
Tallahassee, Florida 32301

☐ I would like to learn more about the **Capital Health Plan.** Please add
my name to your mailing list.

- I am ☐, am not ☐, covered under the state group health insurance
  program.
- If covered, do you have individual ☐, or family ☐ coverage?
- Number of adults _____ and children _____ in your
  household (include yourself).
- I have ☐, have not ☐ purchased supplemental health insurance at
  work.
- How important do you feel your personal involvement is in this
  issue? ☐ not important ☐ somewhat important ☐ very important

_____

(Name)

_____

(Address)

_____

Logistical Considerations in the Prepaid Health Industry: An Exploratory Analysis

Robert E. Sweeney
James P. Rakowski

I. INTRODUCTION

This article will provide a general introduction to logistical factors in a growth service industry: prepaid health care. Prepaid health care can be casually defined for the purposes of this presentation as any *service* environment where the provider institution(s) delivers health care services in exchange for a fixed monthly fee paid in advance of the insurance period. The services delivered, typically including basic, hospital, major medical and preventive care coverages, may be provided by a variety of organizations. The organizations may be commercial insurance companies, Blue Cross/Blue Shield, welfare trust funds of organized labor, corporations, Health Maintenance Organizations or any of several alternative delivery systems.

This presentation will focus on logistical issues concerning the type of delivery system known as the Health Maintenance Organization (HMO). The source materials include published literature, formal and informal materials from several operational HMOs, communications with expert management in the prepaid health industry, and one of the author's four years of experience as a consultant and manager in two different HMOs. There is very little published on logistics theory and practice for service or intangible goods industries. Therefore, much of what follows should be taken in the vein of suggestion or hypothesis subject to future confirmation and testing.

Robert E. Sweeney is Instructor in Marketing, Memphis State University, and James P. Rakowski is Professor of Transportation and Logistics, Memphis State University.

A full treatment of service logistics in the HMO environment would have to touch upon a minimum of the following topics:

1. Organizational/structural alternatives
2. MIS and system controls
3. Order and information flows
4. Site selection
5. Benefit/product development
6. Pricing
7. Inventory control
8. Regulatory constraints
9. Customer satisfaction

Many of these topics will be addressed to some extent in the following discussions, but the analysis will be integrated into a general development of two themes:

1. The nature of the cost-service tradeoff.
2. Mechanisms for measuring, controlling and forecasting cost-service levels.

These are the crucial questions in the day-to-day management of these organizations as they attempt to grow from a vulnerable financial position at birth to breakeven and prosperity. By understanding these themes, one can more readily identify the organizational and functional situations in which a logistical consideration comes into play.

II. THE COST-SERVICE TRADEOFF IN HEALTH CARE

It is a simple, but painful fact that over the last few decades there has been no direct cost-service tradeoff in the fee-for-service medical sector. Hospitals, physicians and insurance institutions for the most part have operated as if human and capital resources were infinite. They have simply summed up their costs and passed them on to the public either via growth of federal support programs (Medicare, Medicaid, CHAMPUS, et al.) or through the third-party payment mechanism which dominates commercial insurance. However, third-party payment has the insidious effect of separating the consumer from the direct financial consequences of his purchase activity by transferring the burden of payment for services to the insurer.

Given the sensitivity of health and medical care issues and the natural expectation on the part of the ill that they will receive only "the best" in treatment, it is little surprise that the public has come to view improvements in medical care as a "right" and to expect physicians and hospitals to provide unlimited resources when necessary to overcome illness. In fact, for many people, the suggestion of a cost-service tradeoff short of 100% service levels would raise strong fear of impropriety or malpractice in treatment of illness. In short, good care has come to mean more care; more care to mean *more expensive care.*[1] Seldom has the question been asked of whether or not a given treatment protocol or technological innovation is demonstrably effective, or whether the condition under treatment, particularly chronic illness, is amenable to cure by medical technology.

The HMO concept implicitly challenges the view of medicine as a cost-free endeavor and the corollary that any health or medical condition can be overcome by a sufficient application of money, equipment, medicine and physician power. There *is* a cost-service tradeoff, even if only an indirect one measured by double-digit health industry cost increases, dramatically rising insurance premiums, and a growing contribution of the health sector to chronic national inflation. To fully appreciate how HMOs establish and manage a cost-service trade-off, it will be useful to examine more closely the marketing and resource-management activities of these alternative delivery systems.

HMOs succeed to the extent to which they put their physician providers at risk. This statement can be made because national figures show a clear and direct relationhip between reduced hospitalization and organizational control of physician activities.[2] This is an important relationship because HMOs gain most of their economies through reductions in hospitalization.[3]

What does it mean to put physicians at risk? In effect, it means to neutralize or remove the oligopolistic environment which prevents the operation of supply and demand constraints in the fee-for-service sector. In fee-for-service, the physician community has created over the last fifty years a condition of artificial shortage. The shortage reflects both the difficulty of getting into medical schools and the forest of certification and licensing requirements at the state and local level which prevent easy infiltration of ancillary and support activities (e.g., physician assistant) by the general labor force. Specialization is rampant, reflecting a perverse reimbursement system that rewards those physicians and hospitals with the most advanced, high technology skills and equipment. Meanwhile, *as the hospitals compete in an excess capacity environment*[4] for the expensive specialists, primary care medicine has suffered. Many American cities have a surplus of surgeons and specialists, but a severe shortage of personal and family physicians.[5] In fact, this shortage of primary care treatment is a major rationale for HMO development. In a risk-free—i.e., non-competitive—market, physicians have no reason to be cost conscious because the cost of needless or excessively expensive care is passed on, via the insurance mechanism, to a third party. Of course, the insured public ends up with higher premiums and the health sector generally ends up with inflation. But those effects are removed in time and space. In the short-term, the physician is an income-setter, not an income-taker. His training is technology-oriented and lacking in any "bottom line" business skills, and his patient, seeing only his own immediate predicament and having a generous insurance program, presses for more care at any cost whether cost-beneficial or not. In short, neither patient nor physician bears the incidental financial consequences of his decisions.

HMOs overcome this dilemma in two major ways. First, patients are only reimbursed for care approved by an HMO physician.[6] Therefore, they are "locked in" to the plan's medical staff. Second, the physicians are compensated in such a way that risk is reintroduced as a factor in medical decisionmaking. There are three general ways of compensating HMO physicians, depending on the type of HMO:

Model	Organizational Description	Compensation Method
Staff model HMO	Physicians are full-time employees of HMO.	Straight salary, perhaps with bonuses for coming in under budget.
Group model HMO	Physicians work for a group practice which is contracted by HMO for services.	Group receives a capitation fee (fixed amount per member) in advance each month.

Group must do 50% or more of business with HMO if the plan is qualified.

Revenues shared out to member physicians. Group must absorb losses above capitation, but keeps savings.

Individual Practice Association (IPA)

Physicians keep individual practices and offices, but agree to treat HMO patients.

The HMO is a claims paying agent for the IPA physicians. Physicians get usual customary or reasonable fee or an agreed amount, but 10-15% of fees are held back until year-end. Then losses are taken out of hold-back; savings are shared.

The impact of these compensation schemes, in decreasing order of effectiveness is to make the physician economically liable. If the HMO fails or loses money, he personally is at risk. This process of structuring compensation is predominantly responsible for the impressive efficiencies achieved by HMOs in the past few decades. But we spoke of a cost-service tradeoff? Does the service get lost in the shuffle when physicians become cost-conscious? Do HMO doctors cheat on care?

The answer in general is no, for both empirical and intuitive reasons. Empirically, a survey study conducted by Johns Hopkins University of 26 operational HMOs competing with fee-for-service insurance over a 20-year period has demonstrated conclusively the HMOs are equal or superior to fee-for-service in quality of care.[7] This conclusion is intuitively sound as well since, if an HMO physician skimped on care to save plan funds, it would be a false economy. Improperly treated patients would only return at a later date with more severe and more costly conditions. In short, the balancing forces of cost-consciousness and quality care impel the HMO physician to a delicate cost-service balance. The plan Medical Director and senior management monitor this tradeoff via personal communication and manipulation of the MIS system described in section III of this paper.

Let us pose another question. Do HMOs succeed in establishing a viable cost-service tradeoff by "skimming" a healthy segment of the insured population. If, as critics occasionally charge, plans market only to the young and healthy, then saving money while providing high standards of care would be less remarkable. But such is not the case, as even the American Medical Association's Council on Medical Report acknowledges.[8] HMOs draw a cross-section of the insured population. Again, the explanation for this balance lies with competing forces in benefits and sales strategy. The older, less healthy populace generally find the broad, unlimited HMO benefits very attractive. But, they have to weigh that attraction against the need to give up their current physician if they join the HMO. Older people or those who have previously been treated for illnesses or accident are the very individuals most likely to already have a satisfying relationship with a physician. Moreover, a shrewd HMO marketing staff will subtly pitch their marketing presentations so as to encourage good prospects—young singles, couples and families— while discouraging others.

The crucial requirement that management control the cost-service tradeoff is brought out strongly in two types of vicious cycles that can befall the HMO when effective planning is absent. These two cycles are the backlog cycle and the morbidity filter.[9]

The backlog cycle is an HMO timing problem. The subscriber population of an HMO grows as new subscribers enter and declines as dissatisfied subscribers leave. Subscribers have care needs that must be treated with outpatient services or by hospitalization. Since these needs cannot be dealt with instantaneously, a care backlog gradually builds up. The backlog is reduced at a treatment rate that is limited by the number of doctors employed by or under contract to the HMO. For any given number of doctors, the treatment rate can be increased to a degree by raising individual workloads and by employing paramedical people. Beyond that point, however, the care backlog begins to grow. As the subscriber population grows and its demands begin to exceed the treatment capacity of the available doctors, two mechanisms in the form of negative feedback control loops come into play to relieve the strain. The first, and more desirable of the two, is the adjustment of the number of doctors to conform to the care needs of the subscriber population. When care backlogs begin to grow, the number of doctors required also rises and motivates hiring. The rate at which new doctors can be hired may be dependent on the salary range offered by the HMO, as well as other influences. More doctors enable the treatment rate to be increased and backlog to be reduced. As care backlog increases, doctor hiring rises to increase the medical treatment rate, bringing care backlog down. The other mechanism that reduces the strain of large care needs is less desirable because it all but defeats the purpose of the HMO. As the care backlog rises, the delay in getting care also goes up and has a negative impact on subscriber satisfaction. Subscribers sensitive to poor service may leave the HMO, reducing the subscriber population. Care needs go down and the backlog is reduced.

But the two mechanisms described do not always work. If the HMO's administration is very conservative about hiring or contracting for additional doctors, or if patients are insensitive to delays because of inadequate access to other sources of care, backlog continues to grow and creates increasing strain on the staff. A vicious cycle may develop in which the overload causes doctors to begin leaving and the number of doctors declines. The treatment rate goes down and leaves the remaining doctors faced with an even larger care backlog. This vicious cycle can lead to a steadily deteriorating situation in which fewer doctors are available for growing care needs. Such vicious cycles should clearly be avoided by the management of the HMO. Limiting the growth of the subscriber population, or having a temporary source of part-time doctors to provide flexible capacity during the growth phase of the HMO are possible preventive measures. Dealing with situations as they arise, however, is often not enough. By the time a problem becomes evident, anything less than drastic measures may be inadequate. As the subscriber population grows, the number of doctors available may seem sufficient. *However, after subscribers have been with the HMO for some time, they become more knowledgeable of the range of medical services available to them and utilize them more frequently for health maintenance* as well as the treatment of illness. Once this phenomenon becomes evident, it may be too late to control workload by limiting new subscribers. Before any new doctors can be hired, the vicious cycle of doctors leaving and increasing workload per doctor may begin. If the HMO gets a reputation for having a very heavy workload, it will encounter difficulties in recruiting new doctors.

The second vicious cycle—the morbidity filter—can affect an

HMO in either its growth phase or its long-term phase of steady-state operations. If the efficiency of the HMO's operations begins to decline, more staff have to be hired and facilities acquired to serve the same number of subscribers. Costs per subscriber go up and are eventually reflected in higher premiums. People who are often ill and require care may not be bothered by the higher premiums, feeling that they can still get their money's worth; but those who are healthier and get less use out of the health program would be less willing to join the HMO as its premiums rise. Similarly, healthier people already enrolled in the HMO may be motivated to drop out by higher premiums while those who utilize services more frequently will be less sensitive to premium increases. The expensive HMO, in effect becomes a filter, drawing in people who require more care while discouraging and driving out those who are healthier and would not utilize its services very frequently. Average morbidity of the subscriber population increases as a result of this filter effect, and care needs go up.

If the HMO raises benefits to compensate partially for the higher premiums, utilization can go up even further and the HMO may become even more attractive to those who are very ill. Higher utilization creates larger backlogs and greater resource requirements, especially for more doctors. As doctors are hired and other resources acquired, costs go up and force premiums higher to complete the cycle.

Two strategies can be employed to avoid or get out of this vicious cycle. The HMO should have a cost-accounting system that reveals whether excessive cost increases are due to operating inefficiencies, or are caused by a rising average morbidity among the subscriber population. If inefficient operations are revealed as the cause of rising costs, a strategy should be developed that focuses on cost control and allocates more effort to cost-saving studies, measures to improve efficiency, and the introduction of labor-saving technology.

If the HMO's costs seem to be rising because it is serving a higher cost population, a strategy of selective marketing is in order. Selective marketing can be carried out in several ways. Efforts to stimulate new enrollment can be directed at groups that are expected to contain mostly low utilizers. Experience rating under which low utilizer groups are offered lower premiums would be another way of overcoming high utilization problems, but this option is not available by law to qualified HMOs. Adjustment of the benefit package in a way that would not affect low utilizers very much but would discourage high utilizers is a third alternative. The use of at least one of these alternatives may be necessary if the rising average morbidity-high cost cycle is to be avoided.

III. MANAGEMENT INFORMATION SYSTEM AND SYSTEM OF CONTROLS

The preceding section described the scarce resource environment in which HMO management operates and the ongoing effort to balance cost and service in a high risk financial atmosphere. This section investigates the mechanisms by which the HMO manager collects information necessary for planning and corrective action. It also describes the system of controls which permits management to forestall severe problems, coordinate marketing and health delivery activities, and meet internal and external reporting standards. Unsurprisingly, much of the focus of control exercised by senior management is situated in the Finance Department. That's because finance is commonly the "neutral" arbiter of cost-service conflicts between Marketing and Health Services Delivery and also because many of the reporting requirements are financial in nature.

The following presentation is a synthetic description. One of the co-authors was one of two individuals with primary responsibility for designing the original management information system (MIS) and control mechanisms for a major HMO in the Southeastern U.S. The general intention is to leave the reader with an impression of how internal control mechanisms are developed and used to provide crucial information. This impression should be suggestive of how other service institutions might approach information needs and how they might foresee and resolve problems of a logistical nature.

In developing a management information system (MIS), the organization should begin by developing system objectives. Among the most important objectives to be satisfied by MIS for HMO management are:

— *User Orientation:* The system should be structured around the HMO's internal management needs. The system design features should be oriented to the particular needs of key users. A by-product should be the ability to produce external reports, including National Reporting Requirements for the Office of

Health Maintenance Organizations (OHMO) in Washington, D.C., if necessary.

—*Expandable:* The system should be able to be expanded easily to meet the growing transaction processing needs associated with increasing enrollment levels.

—*Comprehensiveness:* Information should support the full spectrum of management functions:

- —Planning
- —Budgeting
- —Enrollment
- —Accounting
- —Patient Care and Utilization
- —Evaluation

—*Flexible/Modular:* The system should be configured in such a manner as to minimize the financial and operational impact of both internal and external changes. It should have a flexible, efficient, and modular logic structure that permits new modules or applications to be incorporated into the overall system configuration without necessitating extensive conceptual design changes.

—*Integrated Design Approach:* The system should allow for interface of different modules, sharing of common data elements, and consolidated reporting of management data.

—*Efficient:* The system should increase efficiency by minimizing the data collection and processing burden on clinical staff; avoiding duplication of effort; eliminating untimely delays in schedules, rosters, bills and other data; minimizing the resources necessary for program operations; and otherwise increasing the efficiency of the HMO.

—*Cost-Effective:* The cost of the system must be in line with the HMO's need for information at various stages of development.

—*Reliable:* The system must provide extensive checks on the quality of the data input. The system should also have processing safeguards to assure report accuracy.

—*Timely:* The MIS must produce reliable data on a timely basis. Management must be able to specify the plan's operational and financial status at any time.

—*Controllable:* The system should be controlled by management. The HMO is accountable financially, professionally, and contractually for the provision of health care services to its enrolled population. Therefore, the HMO must be able to control the data for accuracy, reliability and timeliness.

In concert with these objectives, several HMOs have opted for an MIS that is initially manual and then is phased into automated status as membership and utilization grow. Automation is phased in by module:

—Enrollment and membership data are usually automated first;
—Utilization is automated at the same time as enrollment, or shortly thereafter;
—Planning, budgeting, and accounting systems are the last to be automated.

These priorities correspond to the anticipated transaction volume. Modules with the highest volume are automated first.

There are several significant strengths to the "initial manual, then phased automation" approach:

—The operations of the manual system are simple and efficient as well as much less expensive than automated data processing. This is an important consideration in the early days of operation when revenues are small and the management team is still on the learning curve.
—Experience gained by management in the early stages of development helps to better indicate long-term data system needs, thereby alleviating costly, time-consuming changes to an automated system.
—The MIS may be automated more readily as increased processing volumes and information needs warrant a mechanized system. Phasing avoids long intervals of "dead" time when manual is being replaced by an automated system.

The system is developed considering management needs for information throughout the fiscal and management cycles. The remainder of this section presents an analysis of the relevant aspects of HMO organization structure and how the MIS interacts with this structure.

Critical organization factors influencing MIS design include the mix of the serviced population, source of funds, services provided, and the method of providing services. Figure 1 schematically presents these organizational components. Let us examine each in more detail.

1. *HMO plans to service a population composed primarily of prepaid members, with a small number of fee-for-service patients.*
   The HMO patient load will be composed primarily of prepaid members. Although the goal of the organization is to provide service mainly on a prepaid basis to employer groups, additional patients will be provided care on a prepaid non-group and fee-for-service basis. Based on initial projections of the population mix, the initially manual MIS must provide the proper procedures to respond to three types of patients:

   — Prepaid employer groups
   — Prepaid non-group members, who initially joined as participants in employer groups
   — Fee-for-service

   Once operational, the fully automated MIS which the HMO will have in a few years will also be able to accommodate other types of patients:

   — Prepaid open enrollment
   — Medicare: prepaid and fee-for-service
   — Medicaid

   Detailed operating procedures, data accumulation, and reporting processes must be considered for the initial three types of patients, so that the initial manual system will enable HMO management to properly respond to problems and opportunities.

2. *The HMO's sources of funds are operations and a federal loan.*
   Other than the receipts from prepaid members, fee-for-service patients and coordination of benefits, often the HMO's only funding is a federal operating loan.

3. *A single comprehensive benefit package is offered to the membership.*
   The HMO offers a single comprehensive benefit package to its membership during the period of the manual MIS. This package includes:

FIGURE 1

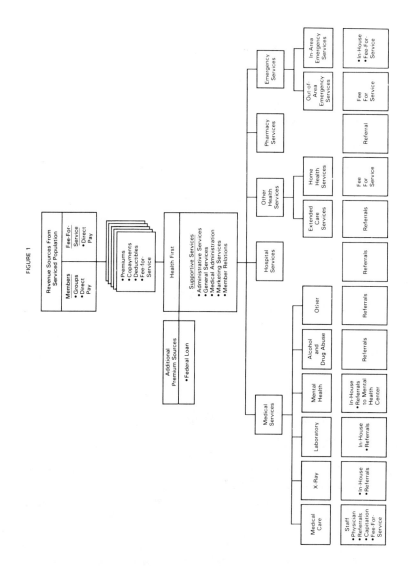

127

—Outpatient care
—X-ray and laboratory service
—Emergency service
—Hospital care
—Out-of-area emergency
—Mental health services
—Pharmacy

There may be specific co-payments and deductibles.

The benefits offered by the HMO and the variety of co-payments and deductibles are fully reflected in the design of the MIS and in the supporting operating procedures.

If marketing determines that it is necessary to establish non-standard benefits, through a rider to the basic plan, the manual MIS should be capable of tracing the utilization and costs of such benefits.

4. *The HMO provides service to its membership, utilizing a mix of internal and external providers.*

One HMO provides services to its member population primarily utilizing staff personnel. Another HMO employs the services of a group practice which contracts with the HMO for most of its business. However, both plans also utilize hospitals, specialist physicians, x-ray and laboratory facilities, and special service organizations to provide care economically to their membership. Consequently, it is necessary to enter into agreements with external physicians and other provider groups:

a. *Referral physicians*: HMOs enter into agreements with specialists in one of two ways;
   Fee-For-Service: Each physician is reimbursed based upon a predetermined rate schedule for specific services provided to members.
   Capitation: Each physician is compensated at a monthly rate per member.

The rates are set depending on the anticipated costs for providing the service, and are updated annually based on the actual and projected future utilization of the services.

b. *Laboratory*: Many HMOs, particularly in the early years, contract for basic laboratory services to be provided in-house. The same provider firm conducts special procedures in its central lab. Initially, charges are on a fee-for-service basis, with capitation a possibility as the HMO grows.

c. *X-ray*: Films taken in-house are interpreted by a capitated physician. Contract studies are usually made at the office of the same radiologist. Infrequent specialty procedures are performed by physicians on a fee-for-service basis.

d. *Mental Health Service*: This service is commonly provided by a local community mental health center on a referral basis. The cost is usually capitated.

e. *Physical Therapy*: Services for physical therapy are usually referred to outside providers.

f. *Pharmacy*: The pharmaceutical needs of the membership can be provided by privately owned pharmacies or by the HMO's in-house pharmacy if the membership is large enough. The pharmacy benefit may be based on a capitation contract or an indemnity plan (deductible plus coinsurance). Walgreen is the major vendor of these types of contracts. Alternatively, the HMO may go to a third party payor, such as Pharmaceutical Card Systems or PAID Prescriptions, which administer identification card-based programs.

g. *Home Health and Extended Care*: These services are usually provided on a fee-for-service basis.

h. *Dental Service*: Dental Surgery and related dental services resulting from accidents are provided on a referral basis. Few growing HMOs take on the risk and expense of a full dental program.

i. *Hospitalization*: Inpatient care is provided by hospitals on a fee-for-service basis in small HMOs. Bigger plans bargain for discount rates in the hospital services market. Blue Cross/Blue Shield IPAs have a built-in advantage in rating from their unique relationship with local hospitals.

j. *Emergency care*: Emergency care for members is provided at a fee-for-service rate when such services are not performed by staff personnel.

The specific services provided and the methods of providing the services should be fully reflected in the system's expense classification system and in the detailed operating procedures used by staff personnel.

In consideration of the organizational characteristics of an HMO, the MIS is designed to provide sufficient data to enable the organization to plan and control resource utilization, respond to third party payors, and develop necessary internal and external reports. These goals are accomplished by integrating the system with the management cycle of the organization. Figure 2 schematically presents the basic components in the HMO management cycle. The MIS is fully responsive to each of these major components, including:

—Planning, programming, and budgeting
—Accounting for and controlling operations
—Providing financial, statistical, and other internal information about day-to-day operations
—Evaluating the effectiveness and efficiency of all activities as a basis for taking corrective actions
—Producing all necessary federal, state, and third-party data required under law or contract

Integration of the information system with the management cycle is accomplished through the development of a classification system, or management account structure, and supporting operating procedures that respond directly to the business requirements of the HMO. The management account structure provides the overall framework for the preparation of planning and budgetary forecasts and for the accumulation and control of costs. It further specifies the functional responsibilities for the HMO to satisfy third-party and national reporting requirements. The basic components of the management account structure (MAS) are the management codes which identify cost center elements. These elements reflect the major classifications for identification of both financial and statistical information throughout the management cycle of the center. They are geared to reporting the outcome of operations in terms of services offered and responsibility of internal management personnel.

IV. CONCLUSIONS

The reader should leave this paper with an enhanced sense of how prepaid group health plans operate, the nature of their cost-service trade-off, and the design and potential appearance of their management information system. It should be kept in mind that the art or

FIGURE 2
MANAGEMENT CYCLE

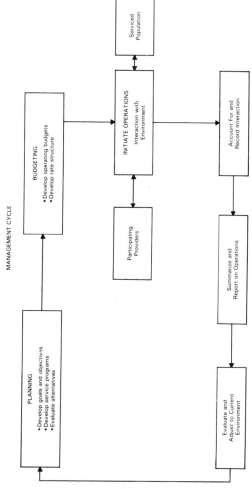

PLANNING
- Develop goals and objectives
- Develop service programs
- Evaluate alternatives

BUDGETING
- Develop operating budgets
- Develop rate structure

INITIATE OPERATIONS
Interaction with Environment

Serviced Population

Participating Providers

Account For and Record Interaction

Summarize and Report on Operations

Evaluate and Adjust to Current Environment

science of managing these organizations is still in the experimental stage and that the shakeout of impractical or financially untenable organizational structures and control systems is still in process.

Since the final verdict is out on "management technology," judgment is also suspended on the best system for managing information flows. This paper has simply attempted to explain how a small group of planners, businessmen and consultants have tackled the critical issue of systematizing the MIS design and implementation procedures. If professional logisticians view service industry logistics as virgin territory, then the logistics of prepaid group health is wilderness within the virgin territory. Any of the focus areas listed in the introduction to this paper could easily justify doctoral level research. An academic interested in carving out a specialty or writing a book(s) on previously untrodden territory has a golden opportunity with prepaid health care. What is more, the industry is both rapid growth and lucrative, offering substantial research funding and career opportunities for those willing to invest a few years on the industry learning curve.

BACKNOTES

1. HMO marketing personnel frequently encounter situations where prospects paying higher premiums than the HMO rates refuse to consider changing carriers because "if my doctor's expensive, he must be the best."

2. See Harold Luft, "How Do Health Maintenance Organizations Achieve Their Savings?" *The New England Journal of Medicine*, Volume 298, Number 24, June 15, 1978, pages 1336-1342.

3. See, for example, the evidence on the seven competing HMOs in Minneapolis-St. Paul published by Jon B. Christianson and Walter McClure, "Competition in the Delivery of Medical Care," *The New England Journal of Medicine*, Volume 301, Number 15, October 11, 1979, pages 812-818.

4. For example, the Memphis area has eight hospital beds per thousand compared to a national average of six per thousand. Such legislation as the federal Hill-Burton Act subsidizing hospital construction and the creation of what effectively is interlocking directorates between hospital administrations and Blue Cross plans have helped to create an environment where all the incentives are to expand because market feedback information on supply is non-existent. In Tennessee, state law mandates that the Board of Directors of Memphis Hospital and Surgical Association (Blue Cross) must have representatives from Baptist, Methodist and St. Joseph-St. Francis hospitals. These three hospitals dominate the local health care industry.

5. For example, the Memphis area in 1980 had only one primary care physician per 1400 citizens compared to a national average of one for every 1000 people, despite Memphis being a major health care center with the world's largest (Baptist) and fifth largest (Methodist) private hospitals.

6. Except in severe emergencies when the HMO center is permitted to seek care immediately from the nearest source.

7. Frances C. Cunningham and John W. Williamson, MD, "How Does the Quality of

Health Care in HMOs Compare to That in Other Settings?" *The Group Health Journal,* Volume 1, Number 1, Winter 1980, pages 4-25.

8. "Health Maintenance Organizations," American Medical Association Council on Medical Service Report, August 1980.

9. For a full development of these concepts, see Edward B. Roberts and Gary B. Hirsch, "Strategic Modelling for Health Care Managers," *Health Care Management Review,* Winter 1976, pages 69-77.

Applying PPO Theory in Maricopa County

Robert Goldman

DEFINITION AND ELEMENTS OF THE PPO

While there have been numerous articles defining the Preferred Provider Organization, a brief review will help clarify the discussion.[1-5] A PPO is a marketing organization for hospitals, physicians and other providers to employers and employee groups. While a PPO may perform other functions such as claims administration and insurance underwriting, the characteristic that makes a PPO unique is the marketing function. A PPO may be hospital, physician, insurer, employer or consumer based and other formats are possible. Of course, each format has advantages and disadvantages. Arizona Medical Network, a consumer based PPO, is competing with PPOs that have been developed by insurers, hospitals and providers.

A PPO is quite similar in structure to an IPA. Hospitals and physicians provide services on a contract under both structures. The primary difference between a PPO and an IPA is that the providers are not at risk when providing services through the PPO. In fact, many planners are looking to a time when hospitals and doctors will offer both a PPO and an IPA to an employer using the identical panel of providers.

THE UNIQUE SELLING POSITION

Authorities have stated that discounting is essential to the success of PPOs.[6-10] While this is true, there is a more important marketing tool: reduced utilization. A PPO must demonstrate overall savings in order to win new clients and retain current ones. Discounts can

---

Robert Goldman, PhD, is Executive Director, Arizona Medical Network, Mesa, Arizona.

135

only save a limited amount. Reduction or even elimination of inappropriate provision of services must be the primary cost cutting mechanism. The physician is the key to successfully reducing inappropriate utilization. If doctors perceive that the PPO is in their best interests, and if they have educational mechanisms such as a utilization review organization or specialty educational meetings, costs will be cut regardless of discount. Without the cooperation of the physicians no cost cutting mechanism no matter how harsh will be effective in the long run. Thus the unique selling position of the PPO is the attitude of the physician.

Physicians and hospitals participate because they see that they must be members of organizations that can compete effectively in the new health care market place. In effect, a PPO is a "Noah's Ark" for providers helping to retain patients. Not until the PPO is operating at close to maximum effectiveness will the doctor see new patients coming to the office. This makes success even more dependent on the attitude of the doctor.

STRUCTURAL ESSENTIALS

Regardless of the format of the PPO, the makeup of the Board of Directors is critical to success. Even within a hospital-based PPO, the Board should be structured in a manner that will permit the PPO to act with some degree of independence. Without this autonomy, physicians will be reluctant to participate. Their perception may be that a PPO is only the first step towards tighter control of their incomes by the hospital. Many doctors, in considering membership in a hospital-based PPO, have stated that they feel the hospital is trying to force them to become employees. Despite the hospital's efforts to demonstrate other motivation, this perception is hard to dispel.

With a degree of independence or freedom of action, the Board and the Executive Director will be able to market successfully. The PPO must be able to build contracts that will have the best interests of the client at heart, even if the providers must make small sacrifices. In addition, the PPO must be able to move rapidly without waiting for the bureaucracy within a hospital to react and take action. An organization with a rapid response time is essential to success.

CHANNELS OF DISTRIBUTION

An effective PPO must be able to market to employers of all sizes. This requires three channels of distribution: directly to the self-administered employer, through the insurance company or third-party administrator and through a multiple employer trust to employers with few employees.

The Self-Administered Employer

The largest employers have eliminated the use of insurance companies and have become self-funded and self-administered. Their benefits manager is in control of their plan and is the person to sell on making changes. You can be sure that this person is aware of the PPO concept but probably is skeptical concerning the effectiveness of PPO's cost cutting potential. While the benefits manager is the key to selling the large company, he or she reports to a higher authority. In some cases the C.E.O. may be more reachable than the benefits manager. In either case the large company will take as much time to sell and implement as any other account.

Marketing Through the Third Party Administrator

A large amount of the market has decided to accept part of the insurance risk in order to attempt to reduce insurance premiums. These companies have a great deal of flexibility because they manage their own benefits packages. They use the services of a third party administrator (TPA) to administer claims, manage the trust account and perform other related functions. The TPA often acts as a benefits consultant to its clients. In this role, the TPA is seeking means to cut the cost of benefits. TPA administrators are aware of the PPO concept and are ready to make recommendations. The TPA should be the first sell attempted. The key to success in this market is preparation. You must have all elements of your program close to being in place while retaining the flexibility to work within the constraints set up by the TPA.

The Multiple Employer Trust

For smaller companies to obtain the advantages of large group economies of scale, a multiple employer trust (MET) is essential. A

TPA takes many small employers and acts as their benefits manager by collecting premiums and forwarding these to an insurance company as if the group was one employer. This saves money for the insurance company and permits the TPA to pass on these savings to the employers. The employer with one to twenty-five employees has been hit hardest by rising health costs. Once the MET is established, this is a ripe market. Usually, the MET will already have a marketing organization in place. Your job is to tie in with this organization and offer marketing support such as brochures, an audiovisual presentation and attendance at training meetings with brokers and agents. There may be times when you will also go on sales calls with agents.

The old 80/20 rule applies with insurance agents as with any other situation. Twenty percent (20%) of the agents will bring you eighty percent (80%) of the business. By working with selected agents, either through the MET or the TPA, you can maximize your efficiency.

Selling the Fully Insured Market

Insurance carriers are also looking at the PPO concept. It is my guess that the standard major medical health plan will be modified, over the next few years, by the addition of a PPO "Swing" option. Carriers will be most selective when dealing with PPOs. The drawback in dealing with these companies is that the lead time can be a year or more. The carriers must obtain the approval of the insurance commission in your state before they can modify their policy provisions. Once this barrier is passed you have the ability to reach all important segments of your target market.

SUCCESSES AND FAILURES

Many of you are ready to market. One of the most efficient ways to prepare for full-scale marketing is to learn from the successes and failures of others. Here are some of each. It seems to me that we all have a quota of mistakes when marketing. The trick is to make those mistakes in a setting that is as inexpensive as possible, such as during a training session.

Do Your Homework

Prior to full-scale marketing, test each element of your organization. The best way to do this is to find a friendly employer, such as your hospital, to work out the rough spots. The use of consulting firms, such as Dale & Associates on the West Coast and Phillips and Associates on the East Coast, can save you a great deal of time and trouble. Your providers, both the hospitals and the physicians, should know the rules of the game and should have some idea concerning when the first patients will come through the system. Be conservative on estimating the start-up date. It is better to be able to move this date up rather than to have to set it back.

You must know your competition. In Phoenix, Blue Cross/Blue Shield is very active. You will probably see them in your market as well. BC/BS has the advantage of a name in the field. They also have extensive resources and leverage with the providers. Their disadvantage is a lack of flexibility. The "Blues" are strong competitors. You must be able to demonstrate that you can compete on an equal basis. Thus, you must determine what position you have in the market and what position you want to obtain (see below for a discussion on positioning).

Another strong competitor in this market is the Medical Care Foundation. With a large doctor base hospital contacts are relatively easy to obtain. On the other hand, it is difficult to be selective when most of the physicians must be included in the provider panel. Tight utilization can be hard to achieve when the panel is too large. Arizona Medical Network has been able to compete with these larger organizations because of the tightness of the medical group and the dedication of the providers to strict utilization standards.

You should also be able to cover the geographical market in which you are competing. In the case of AMN, for example, we have targeted on the eastern portion of the area for direct marketing. Networking with other PPOs is necessary to win contracts from employers whose employees live throughout the greater Phoenix area. Eventually nationwide PPO networks will arise to meet the needs of firms with employees in multiple locations.

Know Your Position

It is essential to consider positioning in your marketing plans. You must analyze what resources you have in comparison to the competition. Consider the reputation and market share of your hospitals. Determine what unique factors give you a competitive edge and what factors your competition is offering. It may be appropriate to have modest ambitions if you are in the initial phase of PPO development. Striving to be the premier PPO in your market before you have all elements under control can be disastrous. In addition, it may not be market-effective to attempt to dominate the market. One legal consideration is the anti-trust laws. By avoiding the total market dominance you may stay out of trouble in this area.

AMN has established itself as the dominant PPO in the East Valley area while not attempting to penetrate the other parts of the greater Phoenix market. By positioning ourselves in this manner, the competition has to deal with us on our turf. Thus, we have a better position even though our resources are limited.

You Must Take the Lead

The providers look to the PPO for marketing leadership. Waiting for the hospitals to develop prices or give other information will slow down the marketing process. The PPO should offer prices to the providers and permit them to respond. Any other system will result in a lack of progress as well as possible anti-trust problems. You may question this when working with a hospital PPO. Even in this situation, the PPO should determine pricing. You will find that the hospitals will respond favorably to this in most cases. You must also take the lead in building a strong physician provider group. One method is to develop a health plan for the doctors and their employees. Many insurance companies refuse to deal with doctors because they fear overutilization. A partial self-funded plan through a TPA can reduce health insurance costs while building cohesion. You will find that the physicians will be grateful that you were active in this area.

Inside Marketing Is Essential

One of your key target markets is your own organization. You must have the PPO employees and the physicians and their employees in your corner. As problems arise, they must be responded to as rapidly as possible. We have created the position of Administrator as the responsible party for inside marketing. Our Administrator is responsible for physician and other provider relations, the management of the office and the Patient Satisfaction Program.

One of the first problems to show up was the issue of acceptance of new patients by established physicians. Many of our providers have full practices. They are not able to accept new patients. We have indicated this in our provider list. This enables these doctors to continue to serve their existing patients under PPO contracts.

A Patient Satisfaction Program should be in place when the first patients start coming through the system. The objective of this program is to solve patient care problems rapidly and provide the employer with accurate information when problems arise. In many cases the employee will have an inaccurate understanding of the system that can blow problems out of proportion. It is essential to respond rapidly and accurately. Protocols for such a program have been developed by most PPOs.

Don't Get Too Big

Even if your PPO has the dominant position within your market, you must still retain control over providers. PPOs are competitive units. They are designed to increase market share for their providers at the expense of other providers. Thus, if your PPO consists of the majority of hospitals and doctors you cannot increase market share substantially. The PPO that controls perhaps forty percent (40%) of the providers can gain market share, retain strict utilization standards and avoid anti-trust problems. In this market the PPO with the leanest organization has the edge. Be selective in choosing providers and do not be afraid to exclude popular, but inefficient providers.

KEY QUESTIONS

During every discussion of PPOs the same key questions are asked. While some of the answers must wait for a few years of experience, I will respond with answers that appear to be accurate under today's conditions.

Q: How many doctors is enough? You should be able to provide a broad spectrum of care within your geographical area. Having too many doctors in a given specialty reduces the impact of your utilization review process.

Q: Why do doctors join a PPO? There are several reasons. At the present time, many physicians see the PPO as a defense against Health Maintenance Organizations. Others see the PPO as a method of reducing health care costs without altering the way that they practice medicine. Many see the PPO as a worthwhile effort and join to support it without expecting to see significant results. For the physician who will retire within five years, the PPO will have little benefit. Still these doctors join to support their younger associates. These varied motivations inhibit the development of a cohesive medical group. You will have to develop ongoing benefits if the PPO is to succeed. Among these are an increase in patient base and fringe benefits such as your own health plan.

Q: Should all of the medical staff be invited to join? No. The PPO is a *preferred* group. Membership must be based on the quality of care a physician offers and the willingness of the doctor to practice in an efficient manner. You must set these standards at the beginning. It may even be a psychological advantage to reject potential members thus establishing the fact that you mean business. At the extremes, there are two points of view. One states that you should have every good doctor in the group. The other says that you should have the smallest number that provide adequate care. You will find that there are several factors—geographic, political and others—that will keep you close to the middle of these two points of view.

Q: If we are selective, won't this cause anti-trust problems? Not if you are careful. The first issue concerns your impact on the market. If you control a significant market share, exclusion from your group could have a negative impact on a non-member's income. It appears to me that there will be enough competition in most markets to preclude this. Secondly, you should develop objective standards of selection remembering that there will always be a subjective component to any selection process.

Q: What about price fixing? The PPO is designed to avoid *price fixing per se* as defined in the *Maricopa Decision.*[11] You will need to work with an attorney who understands the anti-trust issues and is also marketing oriented. In brief, the PPO must offer contracts to each physician on an individual basis. The PPO, not the providers, must negotiate contracts. There must be a separation between the PPO and the providers.

Q: How important are discounts? They are important in marketing the PPO, but not as important as a strong utilization review process.[12] Corporate consumers are becoming aware that discounting may result in false savings. The bottom line is the savings at the end of the first contract year. Substantial savings are the result of reduced utilization combined with discounts. The "Blues" are asking for discounts of up to twenty percent (20%). AMN has contracts where discounts range from two percent (2%) to eleven percent (11%).

Q: How important is benefits design? Very important, but not critical. If possible, the benefits package should be redesigned to include the "Swing" option—that is the employer pays 90% of the bill if the patient uses a PPO provider and only 70% of the bill if a non-PPO provider is used. With many prospective clients, however, changes in benefit design must wait for an anniversary date or governmental approval. You should not wait to implement the changeover until then but do so at your first opportunity. Savings will not be as extensive without the redesign, but an opportunity can easily be lost if you wait.

THE EFFECT OF THE PPO ON HEALTH CARE MARKETING

As the era of competition opens, the PPO will be the fee-for-service alternate to the HMO. Only efficient PPOs who can meet the conflicting needs of providers and consumers will survive. Within five years, most major medical plans will include a PPO option. The PPO will also spur the industrialization of health care. Providers will accept risk where they have not in the past leading to a single health care company offering employers both a PPO and a HMO. National health care organizations, providing comprehensive services, will be fighting over a leaner health services market. In the long run, prices will fall and the consumer will be the big winner.

FOOTNOTES

1. Goldman, R.L. & Reyes, J.G., "The PPO: How to Market It and to Whom," *Health Marketing Quarterly*, Fall, 1983, p. 101.

2. Ellwein, L., "Preferred Provider Organizations: A New Form of Competitive Health Plan?" InterStudy Memorandum, Feb. 16, 1981. p. 1.

3. "Big Changes Ahead In How We Buy Health Care," *Changing Times*, March, 1982, p. 60-2.

4. "Health Care Industry, Business Show Increasing Interest In PPO Concept," *FAH Review*, July/August, 1983, p. 16.

5. Enders, R.J., "The Preferred Provider Organization—Pro-Competitive Alternative or Antitrust Problem?" *Hospital Forum*, November/December, 1983, p.42.

6. Ellwein, L.K. & Gregg, D.D., "An Introduction to: PREFERRED PROVIDER ORGANIZATIONS (PPO)," InterStudy, February, 1982 (revised April & June, 1982) p. 2.

7. O'Conner, M.L., *"Preferred Provider* ORGANIZATIONS: A Market Approach to Health Care Competition," *Hospital Forum*, November/December 1983, p. 16.

8. Rundle, R.L., "San Diego employers behind push for PPO," *Business Insurance*, May 30, 1983, p. 11.

9. Demkovich, L.E., "PPO—Three Letters That May Form One Answer To Runaway Health Costs," *National Journal*, June 4, 1983, p. 1176.

10. Waldholz, M., *"Discount Medicine* To Attract Patients, Doctors and Hospitals Cut Prices to Groups," *The Wall Street Journal*, November 22, 1983, p. 1.

11. ARIZONA v. MARICOPA COUNTY MEDICAL SOCIETY, 102 Sup.Ct.Rptr. 2466 (1982).

12. Perler, J.M., Utilization Review for the PPO," *Hospital Forum*, November/December, 1983, p. 23 ff.

Marketing of Health Insurance Services

Weldon L. Smith
Vinay Kothari

INTRODUCTION

Insurance is basically a service. As Blum[1] points out, one cannot talk about insurance without mentioning service, because service is all that insurance companies have to offer to those who seek protection. In planning for protection or security, whether personal or institutional, a person evaluates the chances of loss and decides whether to take a particular risk, to attempt to minimize risk, or to avoid risk entirely. If the individual takes a risk, either because it is unavoidable or because it is essential to the objective of the individual, he will usually attempt to maximize security by reducing the chance of loss, or taking countermeasures, or by transferring his risk to others through the use of insurance.

In institutions of higher education, health insurance coverages are used to transfer risks facing faculty, staff, and their families. The organization has to provide effective protection plans in order to attract and retain the most qualified people so that it can successfully accomplish it missions, such as the dissemination of knowledge and the extension of the frontiers of knowledge. Organizational insur-

Weldon L. Smith, PhD, CPCU, CLU, is Associate Professor of Finance at Stephen F. Austin State University, Nacogdoches, Texas. Dr. Smith holds a BBA in Insurance from North Texas State University, an MBA from East Texas State University, and a PhD from Texas A & M University. Prior to his appointment at Stephen F. Austin University, he was in the life and property and casualty insurance business for several years. He has extensive consulting experiences and has been a solicitor for a local agency for many years. Dr. Smith was awarded the designations of CLU and CPCU in 1978.

Vinay Kothari, PhD, is Professor of Marketing and Management in the Department of Management/Marketing of the Stephen F. Austin State University, Nacogdoches, Texas. Professor Kothari holds a Bachelor's degree from the University of Kansas, an MBA degree from the University of Missouri and a PhD from North Texas State University. Prior to his appointment at Stephen F. Austin State University, he had held a teaching position at the University of Moncton, New Brunswick, Canada. Dr. Kothari has published over 50 articles in professional journals and books and presented papers in various national and international conferences in North America, Europe, Latin America, and Asia.

145

ance plans involve a considerable sum of money and do represent profitable opportunities for insurance companies.

However, in order to take advantage of the available opportunities, insurance companies must design and implement effective service marketing strategies, keeping in mind the characteristics and needs of the institution of higher education, the environment—particularly the laws affecting the state-supported colleges and universities—and many other factors. The understanding of all the factors which affect insurance marketing programs is essential in an increasingly dramatic, multi-faceted, and independent environment; according to Smith,[2] the marketer of insurance service must know his market and all other pertinent factors.

In order to provide a better understanding, this paper highlights certain major characteristics and needs of state-supported colleges and universities in terms of health insurance. Using a case study, which outlines some insurance related events at a state university in Texas, the paper provides guidelines for the marketer of health insurance services.

CHARACTERISTICS AND NEEDS

Like all business organizations, institutions of higher education must provide some kind of insurance protection against rapidly rising medical costs for their faculty and staff. As the medical costs continue to rise, it is imperative that colleges and universities offer health protection benefits which are comparable to those available in business organizations. Otherwise, colleges and universities, where faculty and staff already earn relatively less, will not be able to maintain academic excellence.

To provide the best possible insurance for its faculty and staff, Stephen F. Austin State University, in Texas, a medium-sized university with over 12,500 student enrollment, utilizes a committee. The university insurance committee is composed of faculty and staff members who are appointed by the President. The committee considers and advises the President and the Vice President for Fiscal Affairs on matters relating to insurance benefits. To fulfill its advising responsibilities, the insurance committee must be aware of state regulations affecting insurance needs, must review the performance of insurance companies providing service to this institution, and must also evaluate bids received from prospective insurance carriers. Keeping abreast of state regulations and reviewing the performance of insurance carriers are two of the most difficult tasks for this committee.

Health coverages are governed by the Administrative Council of the Coordinating Board Texas College and University System. The Council is responsible for determining "minimum standards" that must be adhered to in order for the employees to receive the State's contribution to health insurance. (The Legislative Act, known as Senate Bill 95, became effective September 1, 1977, and created the Administrative Council. The "minimum standards" and this Legislative Act was discussed in detail by Smith and Kothari.[3]) The State's current contribution is $70 per month for each state employee who is employed at least one-half time, and it will increase to $85 the next fiscal year. In the event that "minimum standards" benefits cannot be bought from an insurer, the institution must make up the difference in the total premium for each employee and the State's contribution. In the budgetary process for an institution of higher education, provisions are not normally made for subsidizing health insurance premiums.

There are 1,311 employees currently enrolled in the SFA group health insurance program with an estimated annual premium of $1,352,000. This premium includes coverage for dependents of employees, and the employee pays for coverage for his family. The figures undoubtedly indicate how important the university's insurance business is—or ought to be—to insurance carriers.

RECENT EVENTS AT SFA

Recent events at SFA, however, suggest that insurance companies are either indifferent to SFA's insurance business or do not know how to market their services effectively. At present the university has its health insurance with Carrier A, which provides coverage for the majority of colleges and universities in this State, and has been doing so for a number of years. This insurer is licensed by the State as a non-profit insurance organization and contracts with physicians and hospitals for benefits provided. This insurer is billed directly by the providers of services, and the participants in the group health insurance program receive copies of services provided and the amounts paid by the insurer. The recipient of the services is not asked for verification to make certain that services charged and paid for by the insurer were actually provided. In 1982, the university decided to switch to another carrier (Carrier B) after being served by Carrier A for thirty-six years.

By law, each institution must invite bids from insurance carriers at least every four years. Prior to 1982, few, if any, competitive bids were received by this institution from insurance companies other than Carrier A.

The university invited bids during the early summer of 1982, by writing a one-page letter to each of the 467 insurance carriers eligible to write health insurance coverages in this State. Responding insurance companies were mailed the bid packets along with detailed instructions on how to submit the bids. A lead time of about two months was given for interested parties to submit their sealed bids. Three competitive bids were received, and the university insurance committee recommended, and the President approved, that insurance Carrier B be awarded the business for the 1982-1983 school year. The committee felt that insurance Carrier A's contract would not be renewed for the following reasons: First, the claims payments had been slow. Second, SFA employees were concerned about the cash-flow problems of Carrier A. Third, the administrative charge was higher than that of other bidders. Fourth, there was a general feeling of committee members that employees, as a whole, favored a change of carriers at this time. Competitive bids by other insurance companies facilitated this change.

Carrier B was chosen to write the health insurance benefits for September 1, 1982 through August 31, 1983 for several reasons: First, the administrative cost was much lower than the other bidders. Second, a one-time finders fee was paid. Agent's commissions make up a large part of the premium, and by paying a finders fee this institution would not have to pay further remuneration to agents. Third, there was one claims processor assigned to handle this institution's account. Claims should receive prompt attention, and the client should know whom to contact for direct answers to questions. Fourth, computer facilities of the provider seemed to eliminate the necessity for the client to duplicate the work on its own computers. This should result in savings to the client. During this period representatives of this carrier repeatedly assured the university that they were interested in a long-term relationship. Further, the university was informed by this carrier that they had the expertise to assist with cost-containment devices, and that their claims-handling time would be satisfactory. In actuality, the claims-handling time was much faster than that of the previous carrier, but the time was still too long in many instances.

The university was promised in 1982 that the insurance company would keep it informed of changes in the health insurance field, and not once did they do this. In July, 1983, the branch manager delivered the rerate for the coming year, and the university was astounded that this carrier wanted a sixty-six percent rate increase. University health insurance claims were discussed with this representative to indicate that its claims experience did not justify such a large rate increase. It became clear that this carrier attempted to "buy" the business with satisfactory rates for one year in an attempt to maximize gains shortly thereafter. Throughout the year, the university committee was kept informed by the carrier of the claims experience, and it was led to believe that the experience was satisfactory until rerate time. Also, the committee found that the representative was not even aware that the State's "minimum standards" had changed over a year. If this institution had renewed the contract for another year, it would have had to pay an additional $366,608 above the amount contributed by the State.

Upon learning of this tremendous rate increase requested by insurance Carrier B, the insurance committee had no choice but to contact Carrier A for a quotation although faculty and staff members were generally satisfied with the services provided by Carrier B. Time did not permit the inviting of bids. Within two weeks of the request for a quotation, Carrier A submitted a bid that was twenty-nine percent lower than that of Carrier B. The premium quotation was in an amount covered by the State's contribution, and therefore, this institution would not have to fund the health insurance benefits from its budget.

Carrier A convinced the committee that it was not attempting to get business back at the expense of losing money. This insurance company was very firm on the point that their bid was actuarially sound, and that they would not lose money unless the losses are of an unusual nature and amount for the coming year. Also, action by the new top administrators had caused the cash-flow problem to be eliminated. This institution granted the health insurance coverages to this carrier, and to date claims have been handled promptly. The transition has been smooth, and the relationship with this company has not been affected negatively because of leaving them for one year.

MARKETING IMPLICATIONS AND RECOMMENDATIONS

By leaving a carrier after thirty-six years for a one-year period and then resuming business with them indicates that some insurers are product oriented rather than market oriented. Further, some carriers are more concerned with maximizing their short-term gains instead of desiring a long-term relationship with their clients at a reasonable profit.

The insurance industry has persisted in working from the product outward to the marketplace, and this attitude must change. Consumers are more knowledgeable about what they are buying, and consumers are demanding more service and better value for their money. Therefore, the number one task of a service marketer is to know the market. Lack of market knowledge caused Carrier B to lose this university's business after only one year.

Many services can be performed by insurers in helping keep health care costs down for their clients. For example, Sales Through Service (Blum, 1983)[1] is a systematic method that helps build a professional sales business by giving the salesperson (1) an approach, (2) a track to run on, (3) a reason to call back, (4) a client builder, and (5) a referred lead system. This approach underlines that service should be foremost in the view of the insurance salesperson; for without service, the person has nothing to sell. Carrier B failed to provide much needed service to this client, and as a result lost the business. Furthermore Carrier B had failed to understand State regulations and the needs of the client.

As indicated previously, group health coverages are mandated by State law, and the client has little control over selecting the benefit package. The group participants at SFA are getting older and are not being replaced through attrition. A high female content comprises the group, and apparently this will continue. None of these matters was given attention by Carrier B.

Given the nature of insurance products, make-up of the group at SFA, and external factors, what should be the marketing program of an insurance firm on a pre-sale level and a post-sale level?

At the pre-sale level, one factor should be a complete knowledge of the benefits that must be provided in accordance with the minimum standards prescribed by the Administrative Council. The marketer should be aware of the State's contribution each year and gear their efforts to providing services on a long-term basis rather than one year at a time. Additionally, the marketer should be current on federal as well as state legislation concerning health coverages. In promoting their products, marketers should concentrate on making personal contacts with institutional representatives. Further, marketers should be knowledgeable about their products, and they should promote goodwill through advertising. If these practices are followed carefully, marketers should have laid the groundwork for soliciting the business of the institution. The marketer should be aware of cost-containment devices that should help keep the medical costs down for the people, which, in turn, will keep premium rates reasonable for the services provided.

At the post-sale level, marketers can provide many needed services to their clients. One of these may be a cost-containment service. The "normal" American lifestyle, according to International Health Awareness Center (1982),[5] includes many habits that contribute to poor employee attitude, absenteeism, illness claims, sick leaves, and lost productivity. If enough attention is paid to these habits, many medical care problems could be prevented. The American Health Awareness Center's Life-Health Model, as depicted in Figure 1, is a medical service program which can be offered by the insurance firm. This program takes effect before symptoms and disabilities of diseases disrupt the lives of clients. This program addresses an individual's health in terms of exercise, nutrition, stress, dental hygiene, family medical history, and health knowledge. If

Figure 1

The Life-Health Model

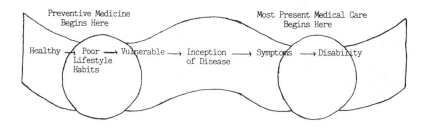

the marketer would provide a service similar to this one, better health should be realized, and the cost of health care should be lowered considerably. This type of action represents a preventative approach to the problem of rising medical care costs.

Another cost-containment strategy is offered by an insurer that focuses on components to effectively control expenditures. The total amount of claims expenditure is directly related to the price that is charged for services incurred and utilization (frequency, types of, and reasons for medical service use). The relationship between these components is illustrated through a Massachusetts Mutual equation: Expenditures = Price X Utilization. The price paid for medical service is a major factor in health care expenditure, and it is determined by such factors as (1) type of service used, (2) type of provider, (3) charges by provider, (4) geographical location where service was performed, and (5) inflation. Utilization describes how a group uses medical services. It is determined by (1) type of service, (2) frequency, (3) type of provider, and (4) medical conditions leading to use. A cost-containment strategy must focus on these components to effectively control expenditures.

Insurance carriers can offer many services similar to those being offered by Massachusetts Mutual.[6] These services could include: First, data collection could be expanded including detailed diagnosis. Second, claims experience could be monitored on an on-going basis. Third, claims experience could be analyzed periodically in order to locate danger signals. Fourth, problem identification and recommendations could be made for specific programs. Fifth, employees could be provided information about health benefits and their role in the medical process.

The carrier can provide cost-containment specialists that can offer on-site assistance and help the institution in many cost-containment devices that will benefit the institution. Taravella,[4] recommends a "Keep Well Health Program" that uses family counselors to determine if the patients could receive sufficient care on an outpatient basis which should lower costs of treatment. He feels that good health should be promoted, and the promotion of good health should be recognized.

Marketers of health insurance service can visit hospitals and physicians and monitor the costs to make certain that the costs are reasonable for the services provided. This helps in keeping medical costs down.

Claims service is very important in medical insurance, and computer facilities of insurers speed up their claims payments. The marketer can provide a valuable service by adopting reporting systems which should expedite claims handling. Simplified claims forms help avoid confusion. The marketer can assist the employees of higher education by explaining the claims forms and teaching employees how to complete the claims forms in detail. With local representation, marketers can assist in day-to-day counsel on insurance questions by the participants.

CONCLUSION

In short, there are many services a marketer of health insurance can offer to effectively serve his customers. A few insurance companies seem to have begun such services. But, Stephen F. Austin University's experiences clearly indicate how insurance carriers fail to understand and satisfy their customer needs. To serve his client, the marketer of insurance services must show an understanding of all the pertinent factors. Providers of insurance coverage for higher education must be aware that in industry all of the premiums for health and life insurance are normally paid by the employer; in higher education, only a portion of the premium is paid by the employer, the State.

State laws applying to higher education are different from industry, and providers must be knowledgeable of these differences in marketing the insurance services to these institutions. Even though the State regulates many aspects of insurance in higher education, each institution enjoys some flexibility in such matters as selecting its carrier. The criteria used by this institution in selecting its health insurer may serve as a guide to marketers. Effective marketing of health insurance services for higher education can offer substantial rewards.

REFERENCES

1 Manuel Blum, "Sales Through Service," *Life Association News* (June, 1983) pp. 95-96.

2. Richard Smith, Jr., "Exploring Methods of Prospecting," *Life Association News* (July, 1983) pp. 83-84.

3. Weldon L. Smith, and Vinay Kothari, "The Marketing of Insurance Benefits for Higher Education—The Buyer's Side," *Developments in Marketing Science, VI*, Miami: Academy of Marketing Science, 1983.

4. Steve Taravella, "Florida Comp Pool Turns Its Attention to Health Coverage," *Business Insurance*, (September 12, 1983) pp. 3, 34.

5. "Pulse," *International Health Awareness Center* (1982).

6. "Cost Containment," *Massachusetts Mutual* (undated brochure).

SECTION FOUR: FOUNDATION OF AMBULATORY CARE MARKETING— MEASURING AND UNDERSTANDING CONSUMER BEHAVIOR AND SATISFACTION

The next section investigates the most important aspect of marketing—satisfying the needs of our consumers. Client satisfaction is a personal state experienced by clients who have fulfilled their expectations and perceptions of the services provided. Therefore, in order to satisfy a client it is necessary to understand their expectations of what they hope to receive as an outcome of the services. This relationship is the backbone of demand analysis in health economics for understanding behavior of the consumer. It demands the marketer or administrator to strive to understand how people develop their perceptions and expectations based on their value programming, past experiences, and input from others. A health organization, however, cannot be "all things to all people." The organization must find a consistent level of performance.

The area of understanding why and how consumers develop their expectations is strongly related to psychographics, lifestyle and value analysis. Understanding consumer's values, attitudes, perceptions, activities, and environmental influences, a marketer can target and develop their services to "really meet the needs of the consumers." A truly responsive health organization is one which strives to satisfy the real needs of their consumers. However, many organizations are not "in touch" with their publics and are quite unresponsive. This is usually not deliberate. Most organizations usually do not desire to be unresponsive. It usually occurs as organizations grow, become more involved in efficiently providing the service, and are a little distant from the people they serve. The national bestseller, *In Search of Excellence*, is almost entirely related to

155

making the point that understanding and communicating to your consumer and staff are the base for long-term success. If we do not understand the people we serve how can we possibly satisfy their basic health needs in a community? It is this premise that the next section is presented in the ambulatory care issue. Ambulatory care is usually even more dependent upon understanding the consumer and attempting to satisfying their needs. Most ambulatory care services are located away from hospitals in the community. These centers become "part of the community" and must be very sensitive to the expectations of their publics. The following articles provide some strong marketing tools for measuring and utilizing consumer needs and satisfaction.

WJW

Marketing Medical Care:
The Manufacturing of Satisfaction

Robin Scott MacStravic

There is little question that physicians will increasingly be competing with each other[1] and with other health service providers.[2] This would normally lead to the conclusion that effective marketing will make a significant difference as to which physicians succeed and which don't. In spite of the logic of such a conclusion, however, there seems to be some continuing antipathy toward marketing among physicians. Hospitals engaged in aggressive marketing and advertising have felt the wrath of their medical staff.[3] Marketing has been described as little more than gimmickry, and unnecessary for a good physician.[4]

A strong reluctance to emulate purveyors of soap, cigarettes, and beer is to be expected and applauded in the medical profession. Perhaps more than most service professions, medicine should retain a dignity and commitment to public good over commercial success that prohibits the use of a host of advertising and sales gimmicks. But to conclude that marketing as a whole is either unnecessary or undesirable does a great disservice to both marketing and medicine. Marketing can and should enable the physician to both do more good and do well, and need not entail any compromise in either dignity or service.

Most of the misconceptions that prevail regarding marketing are derived from experiences with the marketing of products. In the pursuit of commercial success, product marketing professionals (or *marketeers* as they are sometimes called) have often resorted to puffery, gimmickry, even deception.[5] Products which offer few real benefits (cigarettes, chewing gum, beer) and brands which differ hardly at all from their competing alternatives are coated in hoopla, exaggeration and media hype in order to overcome the lack

Robin Scott MacStravic, PhD, is Vice President of Planning and Marketing Health and Hospital Services, Bellevue, Washington.

of good reasons for consumers to buy them. Marketing has become known for artificially creating demand for useless, even harmful products as a way of promoting profit over public welfare.[6]

The marketing of services is a thoroughly different challenge,[7] however, and in any case, marketing is a tool open to a variety of uses and abuses, rather than inherently ethical or unethical. Perhaps the best way of defining or at least thinking about the marketing of services is in terms of the management of successful relationships or the engineering of satisfaction. Physicians, like any providers of services, will succeed or fail depending on how well they meet the expectations of their "customers" or patients. In the case of physicians, customers can include current and potential patients plus other physicians, employers and a variety of organizations. Marketing covers all conscious efforts, what is said, but more importantly *what is done*, to establish and maintain successful relationships with customers to bring about their lasting satisfaction.

A previously mentioned critic of medical care marketing argued the inappropriateness and importance of marketing as gimmickry, then went on to recommend how a physician can become a better arranger of satisfaction.[8] He suggested that physicians capitalize on their individual strengths: a friendly, personable style; disciplined diagnostic ability; efficient office management—in other words, become as good a "product" as possible. He then suggested that physicians communicate to patients regarding what they can expect from the medical care experience (advertising!). All factors that affect the patient/physician relationship and each encounter experience were cited as appropriate for evaluation and careful attention. The purpose of such attention is to increase the probability of patient satisfaction. This is precisely the role of marketing.

EXPECTATIONS

The expectations people have for the medical care experience are important for at least three different reasons. First of all, expectations influence whether or not people seek care, how soon and how often, thereby affecting their health and their medical care use. Second, expectations largely determine the selection of provider, thereby affecting the level of activity and income of all providers of medical care. Third, they determine satisfaction with care, and through satisfaction a host of consequences that will be discussed later.

Expectations of the health care experience come second in importance only to the perceived need for care in determining whether or not people seek medical care. Anticipation of successful prevention[9] or treatment often will determine whether people perceive themselves to be in need of medical care in the first place. If difficulty is expected in getting an appointment, people are likely to postpone and even decide against seeking care at early stages of illness or for modest problems. People who avoid or delay seeking appropriate care put themselves, their families and community at risk, as well as deprive physicians of income.

Expectations of alternative providers largely dictate which will be chosen once the decision is made to seek care. Perceptions of differential levels of availability, convenience, quality, cost, as well as personal features related to caring, feeling welcome and the quality of communications will guide the patient and family in making their choices. Though people may be unsophisticated in their knowledge of providers,[10] they make most choices themselves, relying on friends[11] or other physicians[12] in many cases to guide them. Satisfaction with care is largely a function of the extent to which expectations are met during the medical care experience. The key to successful marketing in any situation is to learn about what expectations people have, then try to satisfy them. The major need that brings people to physicians is the need for medical care, for technical diagnostic and therapeutic skills. People rarely are able to judge the technical quality of care offered or given, however. Moreover, they are also in need of a host of interpersonal skills that constitute the art of medicine. Knowing the full range of expectations that bring people to medical care, and determining how satisfied they will be with the experience is essential to marketing success but also to good medical care.

There are a host of marketing and medical reasons why satisfying patient and family expectations is important. (In any other service situation, the need to satisfy customers would be a foregone conclusion, of course.) The marketing values of satisfying patients are pretty obvious—increasing utilization,[13] increasing revenue for the physician.[14] In addition, satisfaction is linked to a number of positive medical effects.

Satisfying patients has been shown to increase the likelihood that all family members will use the same physician.[15] While this benefits the physician, it also promises greater continuity and higher quality of care to the family. Satisfaction reduces broken appointment levels[16] and increases the likelihood of people returning for follow-up care.[17] It has also been said to reduce the likelihood of filing a suit for malpractice,[18] and to improve the speed and probability of payment by the patient.[19]

If that weren't enough, satisfaction will reduce delays in and avoidance of seeking care when needed.[20] Satisfied patients are more likely to comply with medical advice, hence benefit from care.[21] When patients are satisfied that the physician has made the right diagnosis and prescribed the right treatment, they actually report greater improvement as a result.[22] And finally, physicians enjoy their practices more when patients are satisfied.[23]

To undertake the satisfaction of patients as a legitimate and important part of medical care, and to succeed in this marketing effort, a series of four tasks are called for. First, it is necessary to learn what people's expectations or criteria are in selecting a provider of medical care. Second, it is important to learn what people expect from and how they judge the medical care experience. Third, it is wise to design into or modify the art of medicine toward greater congruity with these expectations. Finally, it is useful to communicate effectively with people before, during, and after the medical care experience.

Market research is the usual term applied to gathering facts about the perceived needs, knowledge, attitude and behavior of people relative to a given product or service. A wide variety of techniques are available ranging from simple group discussions to complex surveys and statistical analysis. Without going into detail about such techniques, they are designed to identify what motivates people to seek a given service, and determine how they choose a provider.

SELECTION

Based on dozens of research efforts aimed at uncovering provider selection criteria, there appear to be at least eight main factors that first influence choice of provider when medical care is perceived to be necessary and people have a choice. These are, in alphabetical order: availability, compassion, compatibility, competence, confidentiality, consequences, convenience and cost. What people perceive to be true about alternative providers determines whether they seek care at all and from whom they seek it.

Availability refers to how likely people think it is that a given provider will be there when they need one. People want to have access to a physician who is reachable after hours, if only by phone.[24]

They want to be able to get an appointment right away and be seen in a hurry when urgency is involved and not have to wait long in any case.[25] Their perception as to whether they can reach the physician and be served when they need care is a major choice factor, especially for people who consider themselves to be in need of regular care.[26]

Compassion covers a full range of interpersonal or psycho-socio-emotional factors in the patient-physician relationship. It is usually the major basis for choice in routine and family care situations.[27] People are looking for a physician (also receptionist, nurse, etc.) who will make them feel welcome, will show concern and understanding. To judge who is the best or who is acceptable in this regard, they will rely almost completely on their friends and acquaintances who have had experience with particular physicians.[28]

Compatibility addresses the sense of fit people have between themselves and a prospective physician choice. It recognizes that males tend to prefer male physicians,[29] while females may prefer female physicians when they can find one, especially for gynecology.[30] Minority races and ethnic groups often prefer to go to one of their own, especially if significant language and cultural barriers are involved. Social class and neighborhood can also be important in terms of whether people feel they would feel comfortable with one provider versus another.[31]

Competence includes general qualifications a physician is perceived to have as well as specific capabilities with respect to the perceived problem that prompts selection.[32] Where a group practice or clinic is involved, the ability to choose one's own physician is a major determinant of perceived quality.[33] Expectation that a physician will provide care rather than a nurse is equally critical to perceived competence, especially if an acute problem is involved.[34] (Once having selected a provider, however, people seem about equally satisfied with a nurse practitioner.[35]) Competence is also judged by the type of location of the provider (e.g., suburbs, nice neighborhood)[36] and perceived hospital affiliation.[37] While the average consumer is relatively unsophisticated regarding medical care,[38] people will also judge on the basis of perceived staff qualifications, training, years of experience and prestige.[39] A recommendation by another respected physician seems to be the most relied upon basis for perceptions of competence.[40]

Confidentiality addresses a desire that most people have that news regarding their reasons for seeking care or information on their condition not become public knowledge. Most people expect physicians and other health care professionals to keep all information confidential except where a consultation is needed. Some people are more sensitive to their privacy than others, and some situations are more sensitive than others to all people. In general, however, people will avoid providers and even fail to seek care if they fear their private affairs will become public knowledge.

Consequences means the results that people expect to derive from using a specific service or choosing a specific provider. Where "need" may be the driving force in motivating people to seek care, it is likely to be the expectation that a given question will be answered, problem will be solved, condition will be cured or other set of consequences that confirm the consumer decision. Where one type of care or one provider is perceived as promising superior consequences, that will make a great difference to consumers. Actually making such promises, however, is considered unethical and increases the likelihood of a malpractice suit.

Convenience is closely linked to availability, but also includes hours of availability,[41] ease of travel,[42] parking, waiting time and other accessibility factors that determine how easy it is to get to the source of care.[43] Expected long waits for appointment or in waiting, examination and treatment areas would be negative factors. For those who consider themselves to be in fair health, convenience seems to be of top importance, where those who think of themselves in good health rank compassion higher and those in poor health rank competence higher.[44]

Cost of care, as perceived by the prospective patient, can be critical in decisions as to whether to seek care as well as from whom.[45] Perceived charges are complicated by the fact that insurance coverage, Medicare and Medicaid remove or mitigate concern for the majority of people. Some, however, may avoid seeking care out of ignorance of available coverage or possible credit arrangements. In any case, expected out-of-pocket cost rather than total charges would be the determining factor.[46] Costs also include whatever pain, indignity, or other psychological harm is anticipated, however, as well as economic costs.

SATISFACTION

Satisfaction arises from the confirmation or fulfillment of expectations.[47] Based on studies, it is generally true that people with higher expectations tend to be more satisfied than people with no or low expectations when experience is good.[48] This is equally true when experience is bad.[49] Part of this appears to be a self-fulfilling prophecy effect.[50] Since high expectations are useful in attracting patients in the first place, it is a happy coincidence that they are also correlated with satisfaction.

The factors that have the greatest impact on satisfaction include all the criteria cited as affecting provider selection, though judged somewhat differently. In addition, there are a number of factors that can only be perceived and judged through the medical care experience. The combined list includes availability, compassion, compatibility, competence, confidentiality, consequences, comfort, convenience, cost, and also concurrence and continuity. In the spirit of this long list of "C" factors, *communication* appears to be the most important feature of the health care experience.

Availability affects satisfaction based on how available a given provider has been and is expected to be in the future. This includes availability after hours, on weekends, in an emergency, and the patient's sense that it is alright to contact the physician whenever an important need arises. Experience relative to this factor acts on satisfaction just as perception of availability acts on selection.

Compassion includes the same features as listed in selection criteria, but is judged in terms of some specific, observable facts. The conduct of the physician,[51] in such terms as letting patients describe problems in their own words,[52] listening attentively, showing concern for the patient's family and social situation as well as the specific problem[53] determines whether the physician is perceived as having a ". . . sympathetic awareness of another's distress together with the desire to alleviate it."[54] The use of non-verbal encouragement and signs of sympathy as well as being physically close to the patient during discussion are strong indicators of compassion.[55] A receptionist who knows the patient's name[56] and the absence of rigid bureaucratic procedures are other specific signs of caring and concern.[57]

Compatibility affects satisfaction as much as selection, though personality and experience replace perceptions based on demographic features. People don't like being talked down to,[58] and will react negatively to perceived arrogance. A sense that the provider doesn't really understand their situation will drive patients away.[59] The pediatrician who is sensitive to the mother's guilt over her possible negligence in permitting her child to become ill or hurt, and who can assuage such guilt during the visit would be rated high on compatibility, where one who ignored the question would not.[60]

Competence is judged through experience on very specific, albeit layman criteria. The perceived thoroughness of the interview and examination process has a great deal to do with how competent patients feel the physician may be. Prudence in regard to surgery[61] and willingness to refer to a specialist when in doubt[62] are also interpreted as signs of a competent physician. The physician is expected to be familiar with the details of the patient's problem and to be able to coordinate care with the rest of the system when necessary. Having modern-looking equipment and an attractive office are also signs of competence.[63] Giving specific treatment such as injections or oral medications,[64] doing enough tests and providing a full range of services[65] are equally important.

Confidentiality in satisfaction may be based on whether people discover that their situation has become public knowledge. It can also be judged by whether a patient or family member overhears physicians or employees discussing another identified person. Overheard exchanges in the hospital elevator, a restaurant, or any public place may provide evidence that a given provider fails to respect confidentiality. Given that some patient situations are especially interesting, poignant or even humorous, special attention is needed to ensure confidences are not breached carelessly.

Consequences in satisfaction cover the outcomes perceived by consumers insofar as they are attributed to the care received. Where positive consequences occur too easily or too late, they may be attributed to natural developments or the patient's own efforts rather than the care received. Negative consequences may be accepted as inevitable or blamed entirely on the provider. Satisfaction with other features of care actually tends to increase perception of positive consequences, even as perception of positive consequences increases satisfaction.[22]

Convenience reflects actual experience with waits for an appointment during the care process, parking and travel time. Many studies have suggested that inconvenience, especially as reflected in the time spent getting care, is a major source of dissatisfaction,[66] while convenience adds little to satisfaction. Hours of availability[67] and the length of time it takes to get lab tests back[68] are also cited as convenience factors affecting satisfaction. People's ideas as to what is reasonable in the way of travel time and waiting time varies widely,[69] but convenience perceptions are clearly important in satisfaction.[70]

Comfort includes both physical and psychological comfort with the care situation. Being physically comfortable with the provider's environment, including chairs and other people in waiting rooms, is one aspect. Having one's physical privacy respected and protected is another. The way people are treated by providers and their employees can either make them comfortable or uncomfortable with the experience. Even the way billing procedures are handled can either add or detract from consumer feelings of comfort.

Concurrence addresses the extent to which patient (or parent) and physician agree on diagnosis, prognosis and treatment. This may seem to be an inappropriate criteria, especially since the patient is not trained in differential diagnosis nor familiar with the pharmacopeia, but it is an important factor in the patient's perception of satisfaction, and indeed is linked to the patient's rating of the physician's competence.[71] Mothers, for example, tend to be fairly good diagnosticians, relative to their own children, and are disappointed if the physician doesn't ask for their opinions, or gives an unexpected diagnosis and treatment.[72]

Perhaps because this has not been stressed as an important feature of the physician-patient relationship, concurrence levels are low in practice.[73] However, it has been found that physician-patient agreement on diagnosis positively affects the degree of improvement perceived by both as well as satisfaction.[74]

Concurrence also includes a second dimension equally important in satisfaction—it reflects the extent to which the physician encourages patients to feel themselves to be partners in a joint attack on the problem.[75] This is by no means important or even expected by all patients, many of whom rely totally on the physician's superior knowledge and skills.[76] For many, however, and increasingly as old attitudes change, the sense of being part of a cooperative effort rather than a passive recipient is an important contributor to satisfaction.[77]

Continuity is reflected in two distinct aspects of the health care experience. Whether people can expect to and do see the same providers each time they come for care is perhaps the most obvious and concrete expression of continuity. The extent to which providers are familiar with past visits and prior problems, especially more recent ones, is a factor that is enhanced by good record-keeping as well as good provider memory. A receptionist who knows patients by name, as well as nurses and physicians who can rely on records for reminder are simple but important expressions of continuity, in addition to influencing perceptions of compassion.

Cost has surprisingly little effect on satisfaction based on past studies, at least.[78] First of all, charges seem of concern only when they are substantially out of line with what other physicians charge,[79] or require substantial out-of-pocket contribution by the patient.[80] When people are really sick and need a great deal of care, the total cost can be of concern,[81] but people would generally rather the physician be thorough and have the latest equipment than cut corners.[82] As insurance charges increase the burden on the individual through deductibles and co-pay, sensitivity to cost is likely to increase, however. The pain, discomfort and indignity accompanying care, compared to the value of results achieved, will significantly affect satisfaction aside from financial costs.

In reviewing the factors that affect provider selection and patient satisfaction, a clear suggestion emerges as to the critical importance of *communication.* Competence is largely perceived in terms of thorough interviewing or listening skills and explanation of diagnosis, prognosis and therapy. Compassion is expressed and judged almost entirely through verbal and non-verbal communication.[83] Compatibility is partly a function of how well the physician indicates understanding and respect for the patient. Concurrence will only result from careful efforts to reinforce or correct patient beliefs, as appropriate.

Much of the value or benefit of the health care experience comes in communication. The patient gains knowledge and understanding of the problem and learns future steps to take to prevent recurrence, enhance recovery or adjust to residual effects. The physician's proficiency at communication[84] is highly correlated with satisfaction. Ability to relieve tension if it arises is equally important.[85] On the other side of the coin, ability to instill confidence in the confidentiality of communication, in patient privacy are important to both selection and satisfaction.[86]

The type of information communicated and even the manner in which it is communicated are also important to therapeutic choices. How thoroughly people understand alternatives and the confidence they have in the physician's instructions greatly affect compliance.[87] Choices between surgery and radiation therapy for cancer were found to hinge on the way alternative therapies and outcomes were communicated to patients by physicians.[88]

Communication is also a vital component of marketing. If people are to select the right provider, however defined, they must be supplied the information they need to make the right choice. If people's expectations are to be optimally fulfilled, it makes sense to guide those expectations toward sound, technically competent care as well as respond to their personal notions of what is satisfactory. Communicating with patients outside of a specific episode of care is the best way to build lasting physician-patient relationships, once satisfaction with each episode is assured.[89]

Marketing asks mainly that physicians learn about, then respond to what their "customers" expect. It does not mean ignoring technical quality or pandering to unrealistic and misguided expectations. Rather, it suggests that physician practice respond to those expectations that are reasonable, and especially those associated with good quality care. Where expectations are unreasonable, it makes more sense to educate patients and the public away from them than to ignore them. Getting appropriate medical care from the right providers is the best way to improve health and control costs. Market research and marketing communication can be used effectively to these ends, as well as to enhance the success of physicians who are as good at marketing as they are at medicine.

REFERENCES

1. Paxton, H. "Generalists vs. Specialists: The Battle Heats Up", *Medical Economics*, May 2, 1983, p. 200.
2. Nirschl, R. "Why Doctors Are Losing In The Fitness Revolution", *Medical Economics*, May 16, 1983, p. 39.
3. Holoweiko, M. "How Doctors Kicked Out a Hospital Board", *Medical Economics*, 60:14, July 11, 1983, p. 92.
4. Scroggins, L. "You Don't Need Gimmicks to Boost Your Practice", *Medical Economics*, July 25, 1983, p. 76.
5. Hartley, R. "STP Corporation—The Successful Marketing of 'Mouse Milk', Until . . .", in his *Marketing Mistakes* 2nd Ed., Columbus, Ohio, Grid Publishing, 1981, p. 193.
6. Packard, V. *The Hidden Persuaders* (Revised Ed.), New York, Pocket Books, 1981.
7. Berry, L. "Service Marketing is Different", *Business*, May/June 1980, p. 24.
8. Scroggins, L. "You Don't Need Gimmicks to Boost Your Practice", *Medical Economics*, July 25, 1983, p. 76.
9. Becker, M. *The Health Belief Model and Personal Health Behavior*, Thorofare, N.J., Charles B. Slack, 1974.
10. Newhouse, J. et al. "How Sophisticated Are Consumers About the Medical Care Delivery System?", *Medical Care* 19:3, March 1981, p.316.
11. Wolinsky, F. & Steiber, S. "Salient Issues in Choosing a New Doctor", *Social Science And Medicine* 16:7, 1982, p. 759.
12. Cooper, P. & Robinson, L. "*Health Care Marketing Management*, Rockville, MD, Aspen Systems Corp., 1982, Ch. 3, p. 35.
13. Roghmann, K. et al. "Satisfaction With Medical Care: Its Measurement and Relation to Utilization", *Medical Care*, 17:5, May 1974, p. 461.
14. Wortzel, L. "Some Determinants of Post Purchase Satisfaction Among Medical Care Consumers" in Newman, I. (Ed), *Consumer Behavior in The Health Marketplace*, Lincoln, Neb., U. Nebraska, 1978, p. 80.

15. Kirscht, A. et al. "Psychological and Social Factors in Predicting Medical Behavior", *Medical Care*, 14:5, May 1976, p. 422.

16. Hurtado, G. et al. "Determinants of Medical Care Utilization: Failure to Keep Appointments", *Medical Care*, 11:3, May/June 1973, p. 189.

17. Ross, C. "Returning to The Doctor", *Journal of Health and Social Behavior*, 23, June 1982, p. 119.

18. Sommers, P. & Thompson, M. "The Best Malpractice Insurance of Them All: Consumer Satisfaction", *Health Marketing Quarterly* 1:1, Fall 1983, p. 83.

19. Wortzel, L. "Some Determinants of Post Purchase Satisfaction Among Medical Care Consumers" in Newman, I. (Ed.), *Consumer Behavior in the Health Marketplace*, Lincoln, Neb., U. Nebraska, 1978, p. 80.

20. Berkanovic, E. & Marcus, A. "Satisfaction With Health Services", *Medical Care*, 14:10, October 1976, p. 873.

21. Alpert, J. et al. "Attitudes and Satisfaction of Low-Income Families Receiving Comprehensive Pediatric Care", *American Journal of Public Health*, 60:3, March 1970, p. 499.

22. Gross, R. et al. "The Influence of Patient-Practitioner Agreement on Outcome of Care", *American Journal of Public Health*, 71:2, February 1981, p. 127.

23. Weinberger, M. et al. "The Impact of Clinical Encounter Events on Patient and Physician Satisfaction", *Social Science and Medicine*, 15E, August 1981, p. 239.

24. Di Matteo, M. "Predicting Patient Satisfaction from Physicians' Non-Verbal Communication Skills", *Medical Care*, 18:4, April 1980, p. 376.

25. Parker, B. & Srinivasan,V. "A Consumer Preference Approach to The Planning of Rural Primary Health-Care Facilities", *Operations Research*, 24:5, Sep/Oct 1976, p. 991.

26. Gray, L. "Consumer Satisfaction With Physician-Provided Service", *Social Science and Medicine*, 14A, January 1980, p. 65.

27. Steiber, S. & Boscarino, J. "Profiling the Health Service Shopper", *Hospitals*, 57:4, February 16, 1983, p. 36.

28. Cooper, P. & Robinson, L. *Health Care Marketing Management*, Rockville, MD., Aspen Systems Corp., 1982, Ch. 3, p. 35.

29. Donabedian, A. *Aspects of Medical Care Administration*, Cambridge, Mass., Harvard U. Press, 1973.

30. Haar, E. et al. "Factors Related to Preference for a Female Gynecologist", *Medical Care*, 13:9, September 1975, p. 782.

31. Kasanoff, D. "Why Clinic Patients Shun Private Doctors", *Medical Economics*, 46, 1969, p. 41.

32. Steiber, S. & Boscarino, J. "Profiling the Health Service Shopper", *Hospitals*, 57:4, February 16, 1983, p. 36.

33. Neslin, S. "Designing New Outpatient Health Services: Linking Service Features to Subjective Consumer Perceptions", *Journal of Health Care Marketing*, 3:3, Summer 1983, p. 8.

34. Parker, B. & Srinivasan, V. "A Consumer Preference Approach to The Planning of Rural Primary Health-Care Facilities", *Operations Research*, 24:5, Sept/Oct 1976, p. 991.

35. Lewis, L. "Patient Acceptance of a Family Nurse Practitioner", *Medical Care*, 14:4, April 1976, p. 357.

36. Neslin, S. "Designing New Outpatient Health Services: Linking Service Features to Subjective Consumer Perceptions", *Journal of Health Care Marketing*, 3:3, Summer 1983, p. 8.

37. Cooper, P. & Robinson, L. *Health Care Marketing Management*, Rockville, MD, Aspen Systems Corp. 1982, Ch. 3, p. 35.

38. Newhouse, J. et al. "How Sophisticated Are Consumers About the Medical Care Delivery System?", *Medical Care*, 19:3, March 1981, p. 316.

39. Flexner, W. "Discovering What the Health Consumer Really Wants", *Health Care Management Review*, Fall 1977, p. 43.

40. Kovner, A. "Consumer Expectations of Ambulatory Care", *Health Care Management Review*, Winter 1978, p. 69.

41. Neslin, S. "Designing New Outpatient Health Services: Linking Service Features to Subjective Consumer Perceptions", *Journal of Health Care Marketing*, 3:3, Summer 1983, p. 8.

42. Freidson, E. *Patients View of Medical Practice*, New York, Russell Sage Foundation, 1961.

43. Cooper, R. "Marketing Attuned to Ethical Concerns Aids Dentist", *Marketing News*, 17:25, December 9, 1983.

44. Stratmann, W. "A Study of Consumer Attitudes About Health Services", *Medical Care*, 13:7, July 1975, p. 537.

45. Penchansky, R. & Thomas, J.W. "The Concept of Access: Definition and Relation to Consumer Satisfaction", *Medical Care*, 19:2, February 1981, p. 127.

46. Ware, J. et al. "The Measurement and Meaning of Patient Satisfaction", *Health and Medical Care Services Review*, 1:1, Jan/Feb 1978, p. 1.

47. Anderson, R. "Consumer Dissatisfaction", *Journal of Marketing Resources*, 14, Feb/Mar 1973, p. 38.

48. Fox, J. "A Different Approach to Sociodemographic Predictions of Satisfaction With Health Care", *Social Science and Medicine*, 15A, September 1981, p. 557.

49. Linder-Pelz, S. "Social Psychological Determinants of Patient Satisfaction", *Social Science and Medicine*, 16:5, 1982, p. 583.

50. Ries, A. & Trout, J. *Positioning: The Battle For Your Mind*, New York, McGraw-Hill, 1981.

51. Ware, J. & Boyle, B. "Physician Conduct and Other Factors That Affect Consumer Satisfaction", *Journal of Medical Education*, October 1977, p. 58.

52. Greene, J. et al. "Patient Attitudes Toward Health Care", *Social Science and Medicine*, 14A, January 1980, p. 133.

53. Weinberger, M. et al. "The Impact of Clinical Encounter Events on Patient and Physician Satisfaction", *Social Science and Medicine*, 15E, August 1981, p. 239.

54. *Webster's New Collegiate Dictionary*, Springfield, Mass., G & C. Merriam Co., 1981, p. 227.

55. Weinberger, M. et al. "The Impact of Clinical Encounter Events on Patient and Physician Satisfaction", *Social Science and Medicine*, 15E, August 1981, p. 239.

56. Greene, J. et al. "Patient Attitudes Toward Health Care", *Social Science and Medicine*, 14A, January 1980, p. 133.

57. Greenley, J. & Schoenherr, R. "Organizational Effect on Client Satisfaction With Humaneness of Service", *Journal of Health and Social Behavior*, 22, March 1981, p. 2.

58. Hurtado, G. et al. "Determinants of Medical Care Utilization: Failure to Keep Appointments", *Medical Care*, 11:3, May/June 1973, p. 189.

59. Freidin, R. & Goldens L. "Patient Physician Concordance in Problem Identification in The Primary Care Setting", *Annals of Internal Medicine*, 93, September 1980, p. 450.

60. Korsch, B. et al. "Gaps in Doctor-Patient Communication", *Pediatrics*, 42, p. 855.

61. Ware, J. & Snyder, M. "Dimensions of Patient Attitudes Regarding Doctors and Medical Care Service", *Medical Care* 13:8, August 1975, p. 669.

62. Ware, J. et al. *Consumer Perception of Health Care Service*, Santa Monica, CA, Rand Corp.

63. Greene, J. et al. "Patient Attitudes Toward Health Care", *Social Science and Medicine*, 14A, January 1980, p. 133.

64. Carter, W. "Outcome-Based Doctor-Patient Interaction Analysis V", *Medical Care*, 20:6, June 1982, p. 550.

65. Ware, J. et al. *Consumer Perception of Health Care Service*, Santa Monica, CA, Rand Corp.

66. Aday, L. "Consumer Behavior in The Health Marketplace" in Newman, I. (Ed.), *Consumer Behavior in The Health Marketplace*, Lincoln, Neb, U. Nebraska, 1978, p. 65.

67. Penchansky, R. & Thomas, J.W. "The Concept of Access: Definition and Relations to Consumer Satisfaction", *Medical Care*, 19:2, February 1981, p. 127.

68. Greene, J. et al. "Patient Attitudes Toward Health Care", *Social Science and Medicine*, 14A, January 1980, p. 133.

69. MacStravic, R. *Community Participation and Client Satisfaction in Children and Youth Projects*, Minneapolis, Minnesota Systems Research, Inc., 1972.

70. Hulka, B. et al. "Practice Characteristics and The Quality of Primary Care", *Medical Care*, 13:10, October 1975, p. 808.

71. Kirscht, A. et al. "Psychological and Social Factors in Predicting Medical Behavior", *Medical Care*, 14:5, May 1976, p. 422.

72. Korsch, B. et al. "Gaps in Doctor-Patient Communication", *Pediatrics*, 42, p. 855.

73. Freidin, R. & Goldens, L. "Patient Physician Concordance in Problem Identification in The Primary Care Setting", *Annals of Internal Medicine*, 93, September 1980, p. 450.

74. Gross, R. et al. "The Influence of Patient-Practitioner Agreement on Outcome of Care", *American Journal of Public* Health, 71:2, February 1981, p. 127.

75. Levitt, G. "Relationship Management" in his *The Marketing Imagination*, New York, The Free Press, 1983, p. 111.

76. Greene, J. et al. "Patient Attitudes Toward Health Care", *Social Science and Medicine*, 14A, January 1980, p. 133.

77. Stiles, W. et al. "Interaction Exchange Structure and Patient Satisfaction with Medical Interviews", *Medical Care*, 17:6, June 1979, p. 667.

78. Fletcher, R. "Patients' Priorities for Medical Care", *Medical Care*, 21:2, February 1983, p. 234.

79. Cooper, R. "Marketing Attuned to Ethical Concerns Aids Dentist", *Marketing News*, 17:25, December 9, 1983.

80. Ware, J. et al. *Consumer Perception of Health Care Services*, Santa Monica, CA, Rand Corp.

81. Kovner, A. "Consumer Expectations of Ambulatory Care", *Health Care Management Review*, Winter 1978, p. 69.

82. Greene, J. et al. "Patient Attitudes Toward Health Care", *Social Science and Medicine*, 14A, January 1980, p. 133.

83. Di Matteo, M. "Predicting Patient Satisfaction from Physicians' Non-Verbal Communication Skills", *Medical Care*, 18:4, April 1980, p. 376.

84. Di Matteo, M. & Hays, R. "The Significance of Patients' Perceptions of Physician Conduct", *Journal of Community Health*, 6, Fall 1980, p. 18.

85. Carter, W. "Outcome-Based Doctor-Patient Interaction Analysis V", *Medical Care*, 20:6, June 1982, p. 550.

86. Kovner, A. "Consumer Expectations of Ambulatory Care", *Health Care Management Review*, Winter 1978, p. 69.

87. Carter, W. "Outcome-Based Doctor-Patient Interaction Analysis V", *Medical Care*, 20:6, June 1982, p. 550.

88. McNeil, B. et al. "On The Elicitation of Preferences for Alternative Therapies", *New England Journal of Medicine*, 306, May 27, 1982, p. 1259.

89. Levitt, G. "Relationship Management" in his *The Marketing Imagination*, New York, The Free Press, 1983, p. 111.

The Effect of
Rural Consumer Satisfaction
on Outshopping for Medical Services

David Andrus
Frank J. Kohout

This study assesses the effect of rural consumer satisfaction on outshopping for medical services. Patients can be considered consumers of the product health care. Consumer satisfaction is an important outcome of health care delivery for a number of reasons. Consumer satisfaction leads to continued use of services, a lower incidence of malpractice suits, and satisfied consumers are more likely to comply with the physician's directions (Ross, Wheaton, and Duff, 1981; Mechanic, 1976; Korsch et al., 1968). Many health service consumers report high levels of satisfaction whereas others report dissatisfaction at some medical organizations (Aday and Anderson, 1975: Lebow, 1974; Ware and Snyder, 1975; Freidson, 1961; Sussman et al., 1967; Greenley and Schoenherr, 1981). Shuval (1970) states that consumer satisfaction should be considered an inherently important goal of health care. In addition, there are practical marketing implications that are based on increasing satisfaction.

Three research areas examined the relation between consumer satisfaction and different aspects of health care. One research area studied the relation between organizational complexity and consumer satisfaction. Although quality of care tended to be better in large prepaid groups than in solo practice (Peterson et al., 1956; Hoffman, 1958; Shortell et al., 1977; Ross and Duff, 1978), some researchers have found that consumer satisfaction was lower in large prepaid, bureaucratically organized groups than in fee-for-ser-

David Andrus, PhD, is Assistant Professor of Management, Department of Marketing, Kansas State University, Manhattan, Kansas. Frank J. Kohout, PhD, is affiliated with the Center for Health Services Research, University of Iowa, Iowa City, Iowa.

vice solo practice (Anderson and Sheatsley, 1959; Weinerman, 1964; Freidson, 1961; Tessler and Mechanic, 1975; Kallen and Stephenson, 1981; Dutton, 1979) while others have found no difference in satisfaction (Gartside, 1973; Shortell et al., 1977). However, Roemer et al. (1973) and Ross et al. (1981) found slightly more dissatisfaction among clients of solo practitioners. Even though there are conflicting results, the majority of evidence indicates that consumer satisfaction is slightly lower in large prepaid groups.

A second research area studied the relation between consumer satisfaction and consumer compliance with the physician's regimen. Research indicated that adherence to a regimen and satisfaction with care were greatest when mothers felt the physician was warm, friendly, attentive, and listened to their concerns about their children (Francis et al., 1969; Korsch et al., 1968). Larsen and Rootman (1976) related consumer satisfaction with health care to the consumer's definition of the physician's role. Other research found that the willingness of female college students to return to a gynecologist depended on how well the physician showed warmth, listened, communicated clearly, and was competent (Kallen and Stephenson, 1981; Needle, 1976). DiMatteo (1979) attributed the formation of this type of relationship to the physician's ability to develop rapport with the consumer. Friedman (1979) stated this required appropriate nonverbal as well as verbal communication. The consumer's perception of the physician's bedside manner, as a major indicator of general competence, was a leading factor in a patient's continuance of treatment and satisfaction with the medical visit in other research also (Ben-Sira, 1980; Cobb, 1958; Davis, 1968; Freemon et al., 1971; Kasteler et al., 1976; Hall et al., 1981; Fisher, 1971; Hulka et al., 1970).

A final body of research indicated that while demographic factors affected compliance and satisfaction in some studies, they had no demonstrable affect in others (Gordis et al., 1969; Haynes, 1976; Kirscht and Rosenstock, 1979; Greenly and Schoenherr, 1981). Consumer satisfaction with health care appears to have a strong influence on how patients enact the sick role. This is particularly true in terms of their buyer behavior.

OUTSHOPPING FOR MEDICAL SERVICES

While marketing researchers have expressed interest in the spatial aspects of consumer shopping behavior, they have not directly examined the process of consumers shopping for medical services outside of their local trade area. Research has shown that much shopping for household products takes place outside of the local trade area (Darden and Perreault, 1976; Herrman and Beik, 1963; Thompson, 1971). There is suggestive evidence that wealthy, privately insured consumers outshop for medical services (Hull, 1983). Interurban shopping for medical services is especially important in terms of competition between solo practices in different retail areas and between a solo practice and a large prepaid, bureaucratically organized practice in the same area. Physicians in a major urban center would like to attract medical outshoppers and, conversely, local physicians would like to keep patients from becoming outshoppers unless it is medically necessary.

Research on outshoppers for products indicated that outshoppers, in contrast to inshoppers, were younger, better educated, had higher incomes, had fewer children, were more gregarious, active, mobile, weight conscious, and optimistic about their financial future (Reynolds and Darden, 1972; Thompson, 1971; Herrman and Beik, 1963; Darden and Perreualt, 1976). Marketers need to more fully understand health service outshoppers if they are to develop better marketing mixes for physicians to reach this market segment. In addition, for purposes of office or clinic site selection and market segmentation, it is important to determine the characteristics of consumers which best differentiate those consumers who outshop for medical services versus inshoppers.

Outshopping has been defined as the number of extra-trade area shopping trips for a given time frame and has been operationalized in a number of different ways. Outshopping has been measured as one shopping trip outside town during the last year, as one outshopping trip in the last six months, as twelve or more shopping trips outside town during the year, and in terms of dollars spent outside the trade area for each of a number of different product categories within a one year time frame (Herrman and Beik, 1963; Thompson, 1971; Reynolds and Darden, 1972; Darden and Perreault, 1976). Sammli and Uhr (1974) maintain that definitions of outshopping should include actual purchases. This study focuses on purchases of medical services from physicians.

HYPOTHESES

H1: Differences in consumer satisfaction with local medical services affect interurban patronage patterns. Inshoppers are more satisfied with local medical services than outshoppers.

H2: Outshopping for nonmedical products and services affect medical service outshopping. Consumers outshop for medical services when they are already familiar with retail services in another trade area.

H3: Consumer satisfaction with local medical services has a greater affect than outshopping for household products and services on outshopping for medical services.

METHODS

Sample Design

The three hypotheses were tested in a rural, agricultural community of 3,000 residents in Iowa. Outshopping takes place in Iowa City, Iowa, a town of 50,000 or Cedar Rapids, Iowa, a town of 100,000. Both urban centers are approximately 45 miles away in different counties. The agricultural community will hereafter be referred to as Rural City.

After a complete enumeration of households was made, a simple random sample of 1,131 households in Rural City and the rural area within a five-mile radius of Rural City yielded a sample of 259 households for a total of 703 individuals. Comparisons with available Census data for the county support the representativeness of the sample. A total of 216 households were included in the final sample. Respondents in these 216 households located their physician in the areas studied. Outshopping is operationalized as shopping outside the county trade area for medical services within a one year time frame.

Interviews were conducted by six female interviewers and one male interviewer, all of whom had extensive prior experience in interviewing. A field supervisor maintained constant surveillance and control while the survey was in progress. Interviewers were instructed to interview the female head of household, if possible, and to interview the male head of household if she was not available. The reasoning for this is that women have greater health utilization rates than men, women have more knowledge about health matters than men, and the proportion of females in a household is casually linked to the number of physicians visits for that household (Cockerham, 1978; Wan and Soifer, 1974).

Interviews lasted approximately 30 minutes. There was a low refusal rate of about 17% based on the 259 household selected. Of the completed interviews, 80% involved a female head of household and 17% involved a male head. The remaining 3% involved other adult female members of the household.

The consumers comprise a generally healthy sample that have few major medical problems. The vast majority of sample members have not lost a single bed day nor work day due to illness. Both inshoppers and outshoppers reported visiting physician's offices for only minor illnesses, such as the flu, cold, and minor lacerations, or for physical examinations such as gynecological exams or blood pressure checkups. Therefore, outshoppers did not base their decision on the need for a medical specialist. Both groups had transportation readily available so they were not precluded from outshopping for medical services.

The Dependent Variable

The dependent variable was the location consumers stated they shopped for medical services. Respondents were asked to state the location of their family doctor's office that they call on whenever a health problem arises. The sample of 216 households was divided into two groups: inshoppers were coded as those who shopped in Rural City or the immediately surrounding area for medical services, and outshoppers as those who crossed the county line, leaving the home trading area, to shop in Iowa City or Cedar Rapids. Of the 216 households included in the final sample, 65% reported they shopped for medical services inside the home trade area. The fact that 35% reported shopping outside of the trade area for medical services indicates that outshoppers are a significant force in the retail market.

The nominal level variable of outshopping was recoded as a dummy variable. Inshoppers were coded 0 and outshoppers 1. This allowed the dichotomous variable to be treated as if it was an interval scaled variable (Zeller and Carmines, 1978; Nie et al., 1975).

Independent Variables

Two sets of independent variables were used for the present study. These included consumer satisfaction measures and outshopping activities for nonmedical products and services. Consumer satisfaction variables with a significant relationship to outshopping for medical services are shown in Table 1. The nonsignificant relations between outshopping activities for nonmedical products and services and outshopping for medical services are shown in Table 2.

RESULTS

The results of cross-tabulations for those consumer satisfaction variables that are significant at the .05 level or better, based on analysis of variance tests, are displayed in Table 1. The findings support hypothesis one. The cross-tabulations indicate that the medical outshopper is more dissatisfied than the medical inshopper with local medical services, the competence of the local physicians, the fees the local doctors charge, the waiting time in the doctor's office, and experiences with other local office personnel such as nurses. In addition, medical outshoppers, compared to medical inshoppers, are more likely to think that the local office does not have adequate equipment, that the health care needs of the local community are not being met and that they should see the same physician on sucessive visits. The consumer satisfaction measures in Table 1 all show a moderate to strong relationship with medical shopping behavior based on the gamma coefficients.

The findings do not support hypothesis 2. All of the relationships in Table 2 are nonsignificant, based on the analysis of variance test. The Phi coefficients indicate that there is either a weak relationship or no relationship at all between outshopping for medical services and outshopping for nonmedical products and services in Cedar Rapids (C.R.) and Iowa City (I.C.).

The question remains of the separate and overall impact of the consumer satisfaction measures versus the nonmedical service outshopping measures on explaining variation in medical outshopping behavior. In order to address this question the next section of the results presents each set of variables separately and combined into a full model regressed in a stepwise fashion on the medical outshopping behavior.

Stepwise Regression Analysis of Independent Variables on Medical Outshopping

The means and standard deviations for the independent variables are presented in Table 3. While many independent variables are measured at an ordinal level, they are for purposes of analysis considered to be interval level. Kim (1975) and Labovitz (1970) con-

Table 1
Percentage Distribution of Inshoppers and Outshoppers by
Consumer Satisfaction Measures.

Variables*	Response Categories	Percentage of Medical Inshoppers	Percentage of Medical Outshoppers	GAMMA
1. How satisfied are you with local medical services	Satisfied	76.0	51.7	.495
	Dissatisfied	24.0	48.3	
2. How satisfied are you with the competence of the local doctors	Satisfied	83.1	63.3	.479
	Dissatisfied	16.9	36.7	
3. How satisfied are you with the fees the local doctors charge	Satisfied	86.2	73.3	.387
	Dissatisfied	13.8	26.7	
4. How satisfied are you with the waiting time in the local office	Satisfied	81.6	67.8	.356
	Dissatisfied	18.4	32.2	.356
5. How satisfied are you with other local office personnel (nurses)	Satisfied	91.9	80.0	.480
	Dissatisfied	8.1	20.0	
6. Does the local office have adequate equipment	YES	70.4	40.0	.562
	NO	29.4	60.0	
7. Do you see the same doctor on successive visits at your office	YES	41.6	20.0	.480
	NO	58.4	80.0	
8. Are you satisfied with this arrangement	Satisfied	51.8	31.5	.400
	Dissatisfied	48.2	68.5	
9. Are the general medical needs of Rural City being met by the local office	YES	54.6	26.7	.535
	NO	45.4	73.3	

*The responses to items 1,2,3,4,5, and 8 were measured on a scale of (1) "Very Satisfied" to (5) "Very Dissatisfied." The responses of (1) and (2) were recoded as "Satisfied" and (3) to (5) were grouped as "Dissatisfied." The responses to items 6, 7, and 9 were coded (1) for yes and (2) for no.

N = 216

cluded that assuming interval level measurement with ordinal level variables did not cause serious statistical or measurement errors.

In order to qualify for inclusion in any model, the independent variable has to correlate with the dependent variable at .10 or better

Table 2
Percentage Distribution of Medical Inshoppers and Outshoppers by
Outshopping for Nonmedical Services and Products

Variables*	Response Categories	Medical Shopping Behavior Percentage of Medical Inshoppers	Percentage of Medical Outshoppers	PHI
1. Shop for groceries in C.R.	YES	4.3	2.0	.123
	NO	95.7	98.0	
2. Shop for clothes in C.R.	YES	48.2	54.7	.061
	NO	51.8	45.3	
3. Shop for auto repairs in C.R.	YES	5.0	4.0	.050
	NO	95.0	96.0	
4. Shop for Restaurants in C.R.	YES	17.0	24.0	.083
	NO	83.0	76.0	
5. Shop for Entertainment in C.R.	YES	26.2	36.0	.131
	NO	73.8	64.0	
6. Shop for groceries in C.R.	YES	11.3	12.0	.009
	NO	88.7	88.0	
7. Shop for Clothes in I.C.	YES	50.4	50.7	.002
	NO	49.6	49.3	
8. Shop for auto repairs in I.C.	YES	8.5	13.3	.075
	NO	91.5	86.7	
9. Shop for restaurants in I.C.	YES	29.1	38.7	.097
	NO	70.9	61.3	
10. Shop for entertainment in I.C.	YES	33.3	36.0	.026
	NO	66.7	64.0	

N = 216

and not correlate with any other independent variable above .30. The matrix of zero-order correlation coefficients indicates that a total of five consumer satisfaction variables and two nonmedical outshopping variables qualify for inclusion in the models for the stepwise regression analyses. The consumer satisfaction model is comprised of the variables of the fees the doctors charge, experiences with other office personnel, if the local office has adequate equipment, if the general medical needs of Rural City are being met by the local office, and if they see the same doctor on successive visits. The nonmedical outshopping model is comprised of shopping for entertainment and grocery shopping in Cedar Rapids.

Three models regressed on the medical outshopping dependent variable are presented in Table 4. An important finding from the stepwise regression analysis employing the full model is that the two most powerful predictors of outshopping behavior are the consumer's perception that the local office does not have adequate equipment and that the general medical needs of Rural City are not being met by the local office. The least powerful predictor of outshopping behavior is the experiences with other local office personnel that consumers have. The asterisk by certain regression coefficients in Table 4 indicates statistical significance for the standardized regression coefficients based on the analysis of variance test.

Comparing the two reduced models in terms of their ability variation in medical shopping behavior, it is clear that the consumer satisfaction model ($R^2 = .170$) explains more variation in medical shopping behavior than the nonmedical outshopping model ($R^2 = .025$). This finding supports hypothesis 3. In terms of the relative effects of each independent variable in the reduced models, the consumer's perception of whether the local office has adequate equipment, if the general health care needs of Rural City are being met, and seeing the same doctor on successive visits are the most

Table 3
Means and Standard Deviations for Independent Variables
in Stepwise Regression Models

Variable	Mean	S.D.	N
1. Fees the doctors charge	1.19	.396	216
2. Experiences with other office personnel	1.11	.319	216
3. Does local office have adequate equipment	1.39	.490	216
4. Do you see same doctor on successive visits	1.68	.465	216
5. Are the general health care needs of Rural City met by the local office	1.58	.494	216
6. Grocery shop in C. R.	1.97	.151	216
7. Shopping for entertainment in C.R.	1.73	.449	216

Table 4
Standardized Coefficients for Stepwise Regression of
Three Models on Outshopping Decisions

Independent Variables	Full Model Beta	Consumer Satisfaction Model Beta	Nonmedical Outshopping Model Beta
1. Fees the local doctors charge	.114*	.110*	
2. Experiences with other office personnel	.065	.084	
3. Does the local office have adequate equipment	.230*	.230*	
4. Are the general medical needs of Rural City being met by local office	.170*	.160*	
5. Do you see same doctor on successive visits	.131*	.143*	
6. Grocery shopping in C. R.	.121*		.143*
7. Shopping for entertainment in C.R.	.120*		.101
Multiple R =	.438	.412	.158
R^2 =	.192	.170	.025

* $p \leq .05$

N = 216

important predictors of medical shopping behavior in the consumer satisfaction model. Outshopping for groceries in Cedar Rapids has a larger affect on medical outshopping than outshopping in Cedar Rapids for entertainment services.

CONCLUSIONS AND IMPLICATIONS

The results indicate that consumer satisfaction with medical services is a major component of rural consumer health care shopping behavior. Outshopping for nonmedical services and products does not appear to have a strong effect on rural medical shopping behavior. One exception to this finding is outshopping for groceries. This finding can probably be explained by the fact that in the areas studied, many grocery stores had a pharmacy within the store itself or a pharmacy within walking distance. Rural consumers who are outshopping for medical services probably stopped at the retail outlets to fill prescriptions. There are highly limited pharmaceutical services in the rural area studied, as is true in other parts of the United States.

The findings also indicate that medical rural outshoppers are very important to the retail aspects of medical services. They represent a large percentage of the medical shopping public. Their number will probably continue to increase because elderly people, who visit physicians more frequently than younger people, are moving to rural areas in increasing numbers. This demographic trend should make the market segment of the rural medical consumer extremely important for those medical organizations that wish to attract outshoppers.

There are several marketing implications that are suggested from the results that medical organizations who wish to attract rural consumers might want to consider. It is important for medical consumers to believe that a clinic has adequate equipment. Physicians may want to invest profits in the purchase of equipment. Consumers could be informed of newly acquired advanced equipment in local press releases. Such press releases are seen in many newspapers. It is important for consumers to see the same physician on successive visits. The consumer thinks that the physician will be more familiar with and interested in their case if they have a chance to develop a long-term relationship. Explaining the physician's fee structure to the rural consumer increases satisfaction. Consumers think physicians charge too much for services. Physicians should also focus on reducing the consumer's waiting time in the office to increase satisfaction as well as have other office personnel, such as nurses and receptionists, appear interested in and be friendly with the consumer. These interpersonal skills can be easily taught to office staff.

Physicians might want to locate their practice near other specialists to better meet the general health care needs of the consumer. Locating a practice near other specialists may create a halo effect in which perceptions of a single physician's competence are increased by being associated with other experts. This may help lower the costs of equipment investment also. Physicians should attempt to locate facilities near a pharmacy or a grocery store that has a pharmacy located within it. Locating near other retail facilities does not seem to affect the medical consumer's shopping behavior. By applying marketing techniques to increase consumer satisfaction with medical services, physicians should enhance the professional and economic viability of their practice.

REFERENCES

1. Aday, Lu Ann, and Ronald Andersen, 1975, Development of Indices of Access to Medical Care. Ann Arbor, Mich.: Health Administration Press.

2. Anderson, Odin, and Paul Sheatsley, 1959, Comprehensive Medical Insurance: A Study of Costs, Uses and Attitudes Under Two Plans. Research Series No. 9. Chicago: Health Insurance Foundation.

3. Ben-Sira, Z., 1980, "Affective and Instrumental Components in the Physician-Patient Relationship: An Additional Dimension of Interaction Theory," Journal of Health and Social Behavior 21:170-180.

4. Cobb, B., 1958, "Why Do People Detour To Quacks?" pp. 283-287 in E. Gartly Jaco (ed.) Patients, Physicians, and Illness. New York: Free Press.

5. Cockerham, William C., 1978, Medical Sociology. Englewood Cliffs: Prentice-Hall, Inc.

6. Darden, William R. and William D. Perreault, 1976, "Identifying Interurban Shoppers: Multiproduct Purchase Patterns and Segmentation Profiles," Journal of Marketing Research 13:51-60.

7. Davis, M., 1968, "Variations in Patients' compliance with Doctor's Advice: An Empirical Analysis of Patterns of Communication," American Journal of Public Health 58:274-288.

8. DiMatteo, M. R., 1979, A Social Psychological Analysis of Physician Patient Rapport: Toward a Science of the Art of Medicine," Journal of Social Issues 35:12-33.

9. Dutton, D. B., 1979, "Patterns of Ambulatory Health Care in Five Different Delivery Systems," Medical Care 17:221-243.

10. Fisher, A., 1971, "Patients' Evaluation of Outpatient Medical Care," Journal of Medical Education 46:238-242.

11. Francis, V., B. N. Korsch, and M. J. Morris, 1969, "Gaps in Doctor-Patient Communication," New England Journal of Medicine 280:535-540.

12. Freemon, B., V. Negrete, M. Davis, and B. Korsch, 1971, "Gaps in the Doctor-Patient Communications: Patients' Response to Medical Advice," New England Journal of Medicine, 280:535-542.

13. Freidson, Elliot, 1961, Patient's Views of Medical Practice. New York: Russell Gage.

14. Fried, H. S., 1979, "Nonverbal Communication Between Patients and Practitioners," Journal of Social Issues 35:82-99.

15. Gartside, F., 1973, Medicaid Services in California Under Different Organizational Modes. Los Angeles: University of California School of Public Health.

16. Gordis, L., M. Markowitz, and A. Lilienfield, 1969, "Why Patients Don't Follow Medical Advice: A Study of Children on Long-Term Antistreptococcal Prophylaxis," Journal of Pediatrics 75:957-968.

17. Greenley, James R. and Richard Schoenferr, 1981, "Organization Effects on Client Satisfaction with Humaneness of Service," Journal of Health and Social Behavior 22:2-18.

18. Hall, Judith, Debra Roter, and Cynthia Rand, 1981, "Communication of Affect Between Patient and Physicians," Journal of Health and Social Behavior 22:18-30.

19. Haynes, R. B., 1976, "A Critical Review of the Determinants of Patient Compliance," pp. 26-39 in David L. Sackett and R. B. Haynes (ed.), Compliance with Therapeutic Regimens. Baltimore: Johns Hopkins University Press.

20. Herrman, Robert O. and Leland Beik, 1963, "Shoppers' Movement Outside Their Local Retail Area," Journal of Marketing 32:45-51.

21. Hoffman, L. 1958, "How Do Good Doctors Get That Way?" pp. 278-282 in E. Garthy Jaco (ed.), Patients, Physicians, and Illness. Glencoe, Ill.: Free Press.

22. Hulka, B., S. Zyzanski, J. Cassel, and G. Thompson, 1970, "Scale of Measurement of Attitudes Toward Physicians and Primary Health Care," Medical Care 8:429-435.

23. Hull, Jennifer B., 1983, "Road to Recovery: How Ailing Hospital in South Was Rescued by a For-Profit Chain," The Wall Street Journal, January 28:1.

24. Kallen, David and Judith Stephenson, 1981, "Perceived Physician Humaneness, Patient Attitude, and Satisfaction with the Pill as a Contraceptive," Journal of Health and Social Behavior 22:256-267.

25. Kasteler, J., R. Kane, D. Olsen, and C. Thetford, 1976, "Issues Underlying Prevalence of Doctor-Shopping Behavior," Journal of Health and Social Behavior 17:328-338.

26. Kim Jae-on, 1975, "Multivariate Analysis of Ordinal Variables." American Journal of Sociology 81:261-298.

27. Kirscht, J. P., and I. M. Rosenstock, 1979, Patients' Problems Following Recommendations of Health Experts," pp. 189-215 in George Stone, Frances Cohen, and Nancy Adler (ed.), Health Psychology. San Francisco: Jossey-Bass.

28. Korsch, R., E. Gozzi and V. Francis, 1968, "Gaps in Doctor-Patient Communication: Doctor-Patient Interaction and Patient Satisfaction," Pediatrics 42:855-871.

29. Labovitz, Sanford, 1970, "The Assignment of Numbers to Rank Order Categories," American Sociological Review 35:515-524.

30. Larsen, D. E., and I. Rootman, 1976, "Physician Role Performance and Patient Satisfaction," Social Science and Medicine 10:29-32.

31. Lebow, J. L., 1974, "Consumer Assessments of the Quality of Medical Care," Medical Care 7:328-336.

32. Mechanic, David, 1976, The Growth of Bureaucratic Medicine. New York: Wiley.

33. Needle, R. H., 1976, "Patterns of Utilization of Health Services by College Women," Journal of the American College Health Association 24:307-312.

34. Nie, Norman, C. Hull, Jean Jenkins, Karin Steinbrenner, and Dale Bent. 1975. Statistical Package for the Social Sciences. McGraw-Hill.

35. Peterson, O. L., L. P. Andres, R. S. Spain, and B. G. Greenberg, 1956, "An Analytical Study of North Carolina General Practice, 1953-54," Journal of Medical Education 31: part 2.

36. Reynolds Fred D. and William Darden, 1972, "Intermarket Patronage: A Psychographic Study of Consumer Outshoppers," Journal of Marketing 36:50-54.

37. Roemer, M., R. Hetherington, C. Hopkins, A. Gerst, E. Parsons, and D. Long, 1973, Health Insurance Effects: Services, Expenditures and Attitudes Under Three Types of Plans. Ann Arbor: University of Michigan School of Public Health.

38. Ross, C. E. and R. S. Duff, 1978, "Quality of Outpatient Pediatric Care: The Influence of Physician's Background, Socialization, and Work/Information Environment on Performance," Journal of Health and Social Behavior 19:348-360.

39. Ross, Catherine, Wheaton, Blair, and Raymond Duff, 1981, "Client Satisfaction and the Organization of Medical Practice: Why Time Counts," Journal of Health and Social Behavior 22:243-255.

40. Samli, A. Coskun and Ernest Uhr, 1974, "The Outshopping Spectrum: Key for Analyzing Intermarket Leakages," Journal of Retailing 50:72.

41. Shortell, G., W. Richardson, J. LoGerfo, P. Diehr, B. Weaver, and K. Green, 1977, "The Relationships Among Dimensions of Health Services in Two Provider Systems: A Causal Model Approach," Journal of Health and Social Behavior 18:139-159.

42. Sussman, Marvin B., Eleanor Caplan, Marie Haug, and Marjorie Stern, 1967, The Walking Patient. Cleveland: Case Western Reserve University Press.

43. Tessler, R. and David Mechanic, 1975, "Consumer Satisfaction with Prepaid Group Practice: A Comparative Study," Journal of Health and Social Behavior 16:95-113.

44. Thompson, John R., 1971, "Characteristics and Behavior of Outshopping Consumers," Journal of Retailing 47:70-80.

45. Wan, Thomas, and Scott Soifer, 1974. "Determinants of Physician Utilization: A Causal Analysis," Journal of Health and Social Behavior 15:100-108.

46. Ware, J. E. and M. K. Snyder, 1975, "Dimensions of Patient Attitudes Regarding Doctors and Medical Care Services," Rand Paper Series No. 5415. Santa Monica, Calif.: Rand Corporation.

47. Weinerman, E. R., 1964, "Patients' Perceptions of Group Medical Care," American Journal of Public Health 54:880-889.

48. Zeller, Richard and Edward Carmines, 1978, Statistical Analysis of Social Data. Chicago: Rand McNally.

Developing and Administering
a Patient Satisfaction Survey

Matt A. H. Elbeik

Patient satisfaction programs are usually placed in the context of a hospital's Quality Assurance (QA) program, which in turn is a sub-set of the Management Information System (MIS). These three elements are inextricably linked to the overall operational efficiency and effectiveness of the hospital. Although hospital Public Relations (PR) is important, the "modus operandi" lies with the consumer, in this case, as a current, prospective, or ex-patient. It is with this consumer in mind that this paper is based. In other words, the concept of consumer satisfaction as a long-term objective provides the backbone supporting the rationale for patient satisfaction programs.

CONCEPTS DEFINED

Patient satisfaction surveys attempt to measure a perceptive phenomenon. To expand, Green and Tull (1978) note that "the terms attitude and opinion have frequently been differentiated in psychological and sociological investigations. A commonly drawn distinction has been to view an attitude as a predisposition to act in a certain way and an opinion as a verbalization of the attitude." Although the terms are used interchangeably, patient satisfaction surveys may be better conceptualized as patient opinion surveys.

Matt A. H. Elbeik, PhD, is Assistant Professor of Marketing, Divison of Administration, The University of New Brunswick at Saint John, Saint John, New Brunswick, Canada. The author extends special thanks to Mr. Donald Porter, Administrative Assistant and Mrs. Barbara McGill, Assistant Director of Nursing, Saint John Hospital, Saint John, New Brunswick.

This paper was presented at the Second Annual Local Government Forum at the University of Ottawa, Canada, May, 1984.

HISTORIC PERSPECTIVES

Although the researchers such as Fletcher (1982) tend to agree that "patient surveys have resulted in positive action for improved service," Speeding et al. note that "patient opinion surveys become instruments of change only if they influence the perceptions and priorities of the changemakers." Thus, information gleaned from patient opinion surveys must be reacted upon, and not discarded as yet another set of numbers exhausted from the QA or MIS programs.

Although the concept of patient opinion surveying is attractive and beneficial, Ware et al. (1978) upon reviewing the literature identified methodological shortcomings in most of the patient opinion surveys they reviewed, leading them to surmise that the full benefits of such surveys will not accrue until satisfaction can be measured with acceptable levels of reliability and validity. This hindrance may be illustrated by the following set of existing criticisms as identified by the author of this paper:

1. All too often, the measurement device (questionnaire) is concocted "in house" and hence the data so gathered is often superficial in its ability to act as an effective management decision-making tool.
2. Aggregate statistics may be compiled by hand.
3. When should remedial action take place: during the survey, or at its conclusion? Are the results slated for individual patient action, or more as a post facto global indicator of the ensuing scenario (per floor, ward, unit)?
4. How large should the sample(s) be?
5. When should questions be altered or deleted, with respect to a change in the hospital's internal or external environment?
6. Questions surrounding interviewer subjective interpretations of interviewee responses under conditions of poorly worded questions or vague response categories.

One could extend this "laundry list" indefinitely, though the problem does not necessarily lie within the patient opinion survey, more than likely within a more global construct, the QA and MIS programs.

To illustrate this required form of synergy, consider the human heart. In isolation, one might measure intrinsic properties such as wall muscle tissue, ventricular flow rates, or extrinsic properties such as blood pressure or pulse rate. All data so collected would impart critical decision-making information for a suitably qualified individual. Nevertheless, this myopic approach would be discarded in favor of considering the human heart as part of a larger support system, the cardiovascular system. This "Gestalt" approach allows for top management knowledge and support for such an important activity; this notion fits especially well when considering the evaluative criteria.

QA EVALUATION

Suchman (1967) isolated the following perspectives from which to evaluate QA and other associated programs, such as the patient opinion survey sub-system.

1. Effort: Time and money servicing the patient opinion survey.
2. Performance: Degree to which effort identifies problematic areas for remedial action.
3. Adequacy of Performance: Comparison of performance with other hospitals.
4. Efficiency: Considers the concept of cost effectiveness by trimming the "fat" out of the budget.
5. Process: How and why did the patient opinion survey work, or not.

The link between patient opinion surveying and the MIS umbrella becomes ever more profound. The stage now arrives to consider the patient opinion survey program in somewhat more detail, in order to address Weaver's (1975) hypothesis that "adequate data and information and poor communications are problems shared by all health care administrators."

GENERATING A SURVEY

Information from a well-prepared research process is useful as long as this develops into an effective management decision tool, and not as a short-term public relations palliative.

Table 1 outlines such a research process, to which the remaining script uses to illustrate the effective use of marketing research meth-

Table 1

Overview of a Typical Research Process

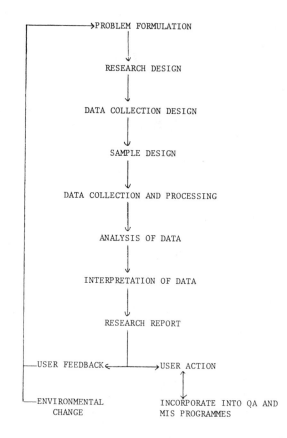

odology as applied to the development and administration of a patient satisfaction survey. The process itself may be explained as follows (taken loosely from Tull and Hawkins, 1984):

1. PROBLEM FORMULATION: The most critical step. Instinctively, a "problem" may accrue when the "ideal" state has, or is not currently being achieved. The ideal state might be knowledge that a significant majority of patients have favorable attitudes toward their care. Alternatively, a collection of objectives might help. For example, to become the friendliest hospital in Canada. Obvi-

ously, operationally defined objectives make the whole research task simpler—the researcher has very specific items to measure.

   2. RESEARCH DESIGN: Depends on what is known, should it be:

   Exploratory—used to discover the general nature of the problem and the variables that relate to it.

   Descriptive—used to investigate the nature of the problematic variables.

   Causal (or, Decision Oriented)—used to investigate the functional relationship between the problematic
variables.

   3. DATA COLLECTION DESIGN:ʼ Where should the data come from:

   Secondary Research—use historic data

   Experimental Research—used to manipulate one or more independent variables.

   Survey Research—taken directly from respondents.

   Survey research may be carried out by telephone, mail or per-
sonal interview. The first two methods deal with past patients, and hence elapsed time from discharge may have dulled their memory. Personal interviews with patients in the hospitals allow for a degree of spontaneity added to good memory retention.

CREATING THE QUESTIONNAIRE

   The issue of creating an effective and efficient measuring device (questionnaire) may be viewed as an amalgam of two component parts. The first is to ensure that the questions do respond to informa-tion needs as requested in the Problem Formulation step. Secondly, the actual form, number, and structure of the questions is best left to a qualified researcher. To illustrate the problems of "in house" ques-tionnaire development, Tables 2 and 3 show the "Admissions" por-tions of questionnaires developed by the Mount Sinai Hospital (New York, U.S.A.) and the Saint John Regional Hospital (New Bruns-wick, Canada). The former went through a drastic increase in the number of questions, whilst the latter hospital tightly reduced its list of questions. Such actions point to a dire need for researchers trained in the the art of questionnaire construction.

   Even though the medical unit managers themselves shape the structure and content of "their" questionnaire (see Table 4, phase 1),

Table 2

Questionnaire Development of Patient Opinion Toward Admission:

Mount Sinai Hospital, New York

"Old" Format
 	
Measurement Scale:
 	
Poor Fair Good Excellent
  1   2   3   4
	"New" or "Revised" Format
	
	Don't Know Poor Fair Good Excellent
	    0 1 2 3 4

Question(s) (1) Admission Procedures	(1) Promptness of Admitting Staff (2) Responsiveness of Staff to your questions about Hospital Policies and Procedures (3) Courtesy of Admitting Laboratory Personnel (4) Courtesy of Admitting Staff

Adapted from: Speeding E.J. et al; Patient Satisfaction Surveys – Closing the Gap Between Provider and Consumer: QRB August 1983, pp 225 and 227.

guidance must be provided by the researcher (Table 4, phase 2). Each questionnaire should include the following:

1. A short paragraph introducing the scope and nature of the questionnaire to the patient.
2. A clear statement assuring total confidentiality of the patient's responses (it is assumed that the questionnaire will be administered in the hospital, for the sake of realism and response spontaneity as per Table 4, phase 7).

The following demographic factors should also be included in the start of the questionnaire. This facilitates the use of correlation analysis and other sophisticated bi- and multi-variate techniques (for example, to ascertain the relationship between gender, age, unit type, and noise level perceptions):

1. Age of patient
2. Gender/Sex of patient
3. Whether admitted as an emergency patient
4. Date of admission, or nights spent in the hospital or a particular ward.

RESPONSE MEASUREMENT

Questions such as how should the questions be responded to, in a dichotomous (Yes/No) or some other fashion? Tull and Hawkins (1976) provide an excellent review of the plethora of "attitude measurement scales." Only two such scales should be considered for in-

Table 3

Questionnaire Development of Patient Opinion Toward Admission

Saint John Regional Hospital, New Brunswick

"Old" Format	"New" or "Revised" Format
Measurement Scale:	
Yes [ ] No [ ]	Yes ( ) No ( )
Question(s)	
(1) Were you admitted through the Admitting Office?	(1) Were you admitted quickly and confortably?
(2) Were you told enough about why you were admitted?	(2) Were you admitted through the Admitting Office?
(3) Were you told enough about what to bring to the hospital with you?	(3) Were you told enough about why you were admitted?
(4) Were you told enough about hospital procedures, etc.?	(4) Were you told enough about what to bring to the hospital with you?
(5) Were you admitted quickly and comfortably?	(5) Were you told enough about hospital procedures etc?
(6) Was your admitting interview held in privacy?	
(7) Do you understand your billing if any?	

Adapted from: Saint John Regional Hospital - Patient Questionnaire 1981 ("Old" Format), 1983 ("New" Format).

TABLE 4

Procedure used to develop a Patient Satisfaction Survey: From

Statements come Questions come Answers come Actions

PHASE OF PROCEDURE	PERSON(S) RESPONSIBLE	ACTION	REMARKS
1	Medical Unit Managers (e.g., Admission, Dietary, etc.)	Provide a list of statements outlining areas of interest for decision-making purposes	This request does not force "question making", rather, a list of problematic areas suitable for question generation
2	Independent Researcher	Designs individual questionnaires for each of the Medical Unit Managers	
3	Medical Unit Managers	To examine "their" questionnaire and to ascertain whether this reflects their areas of concern	
4	Small Sample of willing patients (e.g., 30 patients)	To read and evaluate the questionnaires for question clarity, suggestions, interpretation.	This phase administered by pre-selected and trained hospital volunteers
5	Medical Unit Managers and Independent Researcher	Evaluate results of Phase 4, make any alterations where necessary	Feedback used to develop the questionnaires to achieve a desired level of clarity and comprehension
6	Medical Unit Managers		Finalized questionnaire/unit made available. They may be column coded using coloured paper, or numbered for each unit (to identify wards, locations etc. for each Medical Unit).
7	Hospital Volunteers	When administering the questionnaire, observe strict confidentiality impartially, and accept refusals, do not force completions.	To ensure that all ethical provisions surrounding questionnaire administration are adhered to.

TABLE 4 (continued)

PHASE OF PROCEDURE	PERSON(S) RESPONSIBLE	ACTION	REMARKS
8	Patients	Approached by volunteers for questionnaire completion	Ensure a polite approach.
9	Volunteers	Collect question- naires and hand-in to researcher	Questionnaire coding and computer data entry tasks.
10	Independent Researcher	Use computer package (e.g., SPSS, BMDP, SAS) to analyse the data	The data output should be for- matted in a report structure, ie., easy to read and interpret by a layman
11	Independent Researcher	Develop concise summary stat- istics output	On a monthly basis
12	Administration	Mail to each unit manager his/her summary Statistics sheet	Start of unit decision making process
13	Medical Unit Managers	Communicate findings to unit staff for discussion and hopeful improve- ments.	The "acid test".
14	Independent Researchers, Volunteers, Administration, Medical Unit Managers	Meet once every six months, or on an ad hoc basis to evalu- ate the various questionnaires for inclusion/ deletion of questions to serve points of material redundancy and/or change in questions	To maintain a flexible and meaningful measurement instrument
15	Administration, Medical Unit Managers.	Provision of advanced summary statistics covering the changes over pre- ceding six months (applicable to questions that have not altered over this time period).	Enables administration and managers to identify trends of improvement or indications of problematic areas.

clusion into a patient opinion survey, due to the scales' inherent ease of comprehension and analysis. The two being the Likert and the Semantic Differential Scale. The usefulness of these two scales will be addressed by example.

Likert Scale

The Reasons For My Admissions Were Fully Explained To Me

_____ Strongly Agree   _____ Agree   _____ Neutral
_____ Disagree   _____ Strongly Disagree

The advantage of Likert scaled questions is that they are unidirectional (made up of either very positively or negatively posed questions); the patient merely checks the appropriate response category of agreement.

Semantic Differential Scale

The Reasons For My Admission Were Explained To Me

Fully _____ Not At All

In this case, bipolar adjectives set the possible range of response.

Both scales may be compiled into aggregate scores (mean value for each question), or, into a profile analysis. This involves the computation of the mean value for each of the questions and thus plotting a profile of response (by gender, age, unit, ward. . .).

4. SAMPLE DESIGN: A great deal of literature is available on this rather complex issue (see Schlaifer, 1959; Kish, 1965; Cochran, 1977; Som, 1973)—the complexity arising from questions on sample size. At this stage, the sampling unit must be identified—in other words, will the survey provide information or a per floor, ward, or medical unit (e.g., admission, dietary) basis? Regarding sample size, suffice it to say that a sample of 30 respondents per sampling unit will satisfy the statistical criteria for a standard normal distribution.

5. DATA COLLECTION AND PROCESSING: The questionnaires should be made available for processing at pre-set time intervals (e.g., monthly, every two months. . .).

6. ANALYSIS OF DATA: Although the actual mechanics of survey generated data analysis is carried out at this stage, the selection

of the analytical techniques (e.g., frequency distributions, correlations, t-tests, etc.) must occur prior to Data Collection, preferably during the Data Collection Design stage. Naturally, the whole process is constrained by time and finance availability. One might use PERT (Program Evaluation Review Technique) allied to CPM (Critical Path Method) to design an efficient research process geared toward solving a particular problem.

7. INTERPRETATION OF DATA: The computer adage GIGO (Garbage In, Garbage Out) is quite appropriate at this stage. Firstly, the data must be directly related to the Problem Formulation stage, and secondly, be interpreted with the used in mind (Administration, Medical Unit Managers). The interpretation becomes more subjective on the continuum from univariate (e.g., Frequency Distribution) to multivariate (e.g., Factor Analysis) data analysis. For a Patient Satisfaction Survey, the onus is on user interpretation, and this is easily facilitated if the researcher explains to the users exactly how the data will be formatted for inspection.

8. RESEARCH REPORT: Ordinarily, this is a written report covering a completed research process, keeping in mind that the report be user oriented. For Patient Satisfaction Surveys, the need for a report on the research endeavors should emerge for long-term requirements. For example, how have patient opinions altered over a one-year period, and hence, in totality, have patient opinions been reacted to!

HOSPITAL SUPPORT

As with any change agent, the Patient Satisfaction Survey must be sanctioned and fully supported by all the participating Medical Units and Administration. To avoid suboptimization by duplication, all other QA programs should be tied in with the Patient Satisfaction Survey in order to develop a comprehensive and synergistic QA system.

SURVEY IMPLEMENTATION

Table 4 outlines an envisaged Patient Satisfaction Survey procedure. At the outset, patients and employees must be made aware of the reasons why a patient satisfaction program is underway. As the questionnaires do not pose as inter-departmental ranking devices, (that is, they individually measure different problematic areas), they may be developed and accepted more faithfully as intra-departmental monitors.

The envisaged procedural motions ensure that the whole program has dynamic qualities to it, namely, that subject to medical unit management, questions and/or questionnaires may be deleted or created subject to the demands and interest for decision-making information by management.

It is expected that most of the questionnaires will be administered to patients having spent a minimum of three nights in the hospital (this rule would be waived for the "admissions" questionnaire). Furthermore, the questionnaires could be identified as originating from a particular ward, floor, wing or section of a hospital (by using colored paper, or by stamping an identifying number on the questionnaire itself) dependent upon operations and information requirements.

Each one of the medical unit questionnaires must have at least thirty completions per month for the provision of monthly summary statistics.

Phase 3 acts as a check to ensure that the questions maintain their original demands, and in addition, involves the medical unit managers with a significant degree of participation, and hence responsibility to ensure that a first class job is carried out. Phase 4 acts as a test period, useful for identifying respondent misconception and miscomprehension. Following phase 8, the results are entered onto data coding sheets, and then processed by one of the available statistical computer packages (large computers would normally have one or more of the following statistical packages—Statistical Package for the Social Sciences (SPSS), Biomedical Package (BMDP), and the Statistical Analysis System (SAS)).

Phase 13 is indeed the "acid test," whereby the summary statistics are acted upon by the incumbent medical unit manager. Phase 14 reinstates the need for across-the-board communication to continually evaluate the patient opinion survey, and to modify, eliminate, or create questionnaires as a direct outcome of the hospital's dynamic environment. Phase 15 occurs every six months or annually, and is highlighted by the provision of somewhat more complex and thorough statistical analysis of the preceding data. This turns the "snapshot" monthly summary statistics sheets into a "movie" form, further aiding the decision-making process.

EPILOGUE

Without the continued assistance and cooperation between all the parties involved, there would not be a serviceable QA system. The patient opinion program in the form of a satisfaction survey must be considered as part of the greater system, flexible, and useful—and not an administrative toy to be tossed into a medical MIS.

REFERENCES

Green P.E. and Tull D.S.: Research for Marketing Decisions: Fourth Edition, Prentice-Hall, 1978, p. 109.

Fletcher G.: Another Tool for Better Patient Care: Health Care, March 1982, p. 33.

Speeding E.J., Morrison B., Rehr H. and Rosenberg G.: Patient Satisfaction Surveys— Closing the Gap between Provider and Consumer: QRB, August 1983, p. 228.

Ware J.E., Davies-Avery A., and Stewart A.C.: The Measurement and Meaning of Patient Satisfaction: Health and Medical Care Services Review, Vol. 1, Jan-Feb. 1978, pp. 1-15.

Suchman E.: Evaluative Research Principles and Practice in Public Service and Social Action Programs: N.Y., 1967, Russell Sage Foundation, pp.60-68, 84.

Weaver J.L.: Conflict and Control in Health Care Administration: Sage Publications, 1975, p.176.

Tull D.S. and Hawkins D.I.: Marketing Research—Measurement and Method: 3rd Edition, MacMillan Publishing Company, N.Y., 1984, pp.401-423.

Tull D.S. and Hawkins D.I.: Marketing Research Meaning, Measurement, and Method: Mac-Millan Publishing Co. Inc., N.Y., 1976, pp.334-363.

BIBLIOGRAPHY

Schlaifer R: Probability and Statistics for Business Decisions: N.Y., McGraw Hill, 1959.

Kish L.: Survey Sampling: N.Y., John Wiley and Sons, 1965.

Cochran: W.G.: Sampling Techniques: London, Heinemann, 1973.

Nie N.H., Hull G.H., Steinbrenner K., and Bent D.H.: Statistical Package for the Social Sciences: Second Edition, McGraw-Hill Book Co., 1975.

Dixon W.J., ed: BMDP Bimedical Computer Programs: Berkeley Calif., University of California Press, 1975.

SAS Institute Inc.: Box 8000, Cary, North Carolina, 27511

An Introduction and Application of Focus Group Research to the Health Care Industry

Troy A. Festervand

ABSTRACT. Focus group research is a qualitative research tool gaining in popularity today. An area of potential application for this tool is the health care industry. This article introduces focus group research, reviews the technique from conceptual and methodological perspectives, sets forth a suggested framework for the conduct of such research, and provides an illustrative example of its use in the health care field.

In recent years, numerous changes have occurred in the health care industry to improve the overall quality of services delivered. One of the most profound developments has been the widespread adoption of a marketing orientation and associated strategies, techniques and tools.

Organizations providing health care services have recognized that they can better compete in today's market if they engage in some type of strategic marketing planning. A key ingredient of this planning is the acquisition of timely and accurate information concerning the marketplace. Without such information, any organization, regardless of size, will find itself at a competitive disadvantage.

While various alternatives exist with which to collect marketing related information, this article will introduce and detail a relatively infrequently used technique, focus group interviewing, which has been used successfully by a variety of business firms to identify marketing problems and opportunities.

Troy A. Festervand, PhD, is Assistant Professor of Marketing, Department of Management and Marketing, School of Business Administration, The University of Mississippi, University, Mississippi 38677, (601) 232-5834. He received his degree from the University of Arkansas in 1980. Professor Festervand has published numerous papers and is active in various professional organizations.

WHAT IS FOCUS GROUP INTERVIEWING?

Focus group interviewing is not new, having been used by marketing research firms since the 1950s. Since that time, focus groups have been used in such areas as advertising campaign testing (Advertising Age, 1975), new product development (Ingrassia, 1980), retail strategy formulation (Munn and Opdyke, 1961) and the examination of consumer buying behavior (Axelrod, 1975) to name only a few of the numerous applications. An area which apparently has not recognized the potential benefits of focus group research is the health care industry.

The focused group interview is a variation of the depth interview. In the focused group interview, a small number of individuals are brought together and allowed to interact rather than being interviewed one at a time, as in the depth interview. Goldman (1962) differentiates the two techniques as follows:

> In the group situation a person is asked an opinion about something—a product, a distribution system, an advertisement, a television program, or perhaps a candidate for office. In contrast to the individual interview in which the flow of information is unidirectional, from the respondent to the interviewer, the group setting causes the opinions of each person to be considered in group discussion. Each individual is exposed to the ideas of the others and submits his ideas for the consideration of the group.

USES OF FOCUS GROUP RESEARCH

While the primary purpose of focus group research is to gain insight into an issue or question otherwise generally considered inaccessible, Bellenger, Bernhardt and Goldstucker (1976) note that focus group interviews can successfully be used to accomplish one or more of the following objectives.

1. To generate hypotheses that can be further tested quantitatively;
2. To generate information helpful in structuring consumer questionnaires;
3. To provide overall background information on a product category;

4. To get impressions on new product concepts for which there is little information available;
5. To stimulate new ideas about older products;
6. To generate ideas for new creative concepts;
7. To interpret previously obtained quantitative results.

Advantages and Disadvantages

Hess (1971) notes that relative to other techniques, focus group research offers a number of advantages.

1. Synergism—combined group effort produces a wider range of information, insight, and ideas.
2. Snowballing—random comments may set off a chain reaction of responses that further feed new ideas.
3. Stimulation—the group experience itself is exciting, stimulating.
4. Security—the individual may find comfort in the group and more readily express his ideas.
5. Spontaneity—since individuals aren't required to answer each question, the answers given become more meaningful.

Some of the benefits afforded by the focus group method also represent potential sources of problems. According to Bellenger, Bernhardt and Goldman (1976), some of the more frequently cited misuses of focus group research are the following:

1. The results of the interviews are used as evidence to support decisions that have already been made.
2. Because focus group interviews can generally be conducted much more quickly and cost efficiently than survey research, they often are used for topics not suited for group interviewing.
3. The results of the interviews are used as the only "empirical" support for a given decision.
4. All too often, the sample used in group interviewing is not representative of the population under study.
5. The results of the focus group are tied directly to the quality of the group moderator who may introduce bias into the process.

Because of the criticality of the moderator's role in the group interview, a great deal of attention should be devoted to the selection of an "appropriate" discussion leader.

The Moderator

Focus group research involves a moderator or discussion leader conducting multiple group discussions about a particular subject of interest. Under the guidance and direction of a trained leader, the group focuses its attention on a selected topic. During the interview, the moderator plays the central role of discussion "facilitator" (Keown, 1983). The moderator must not only direct the discussion, but he/she must do so in a manner that stimulates and promotes "creative interaction" among the group members. As Churchill (1983) notes, the role of the moderator is an extremely delicate one. It requires someone who is intimately familiar with the purpose and objectives of the research and at the same time possesses good interpersonal communication skill.

Some authorities argue that focus group interviews should only be conducted by a marketing research specialist or a trained consultant. The major thrust of their argument revolves around the potential bias that an unqualified moderator may introduce via the misconduct of a session or the misinterpretation of its results (Bellenger, Bernhardt and Goldstucker, 1976). Keown (1983) notes that a moderator should have experience with focus group research. The moderator should possess the ability to know when to probe a particular subject/statement/participant, as well as when to "move on". Chase (1973) notes that the ideal moderator should possess seven key qualifications.

1. Kind but firm—In order to elicit necessary interaction, the moderator must combine a disciplined detachment with understanding empathy.
2. Permissiveness—The moderator must at all times be alert to indications that the group atmosphere of cordiality is disintegrating. Before permissiveness leads to chaos, the moderator must re-establish the group purpose and maintain its orientation to the subject.
3. Involvement—Since the principal reason for the group interview is to expose feelings and to obtain reactions indicative of deeper feelings, the moderator must encourage and stimulate intensive personal involvement.
4. Incomplete understanding—The moderator should possess the ability to convey lack of complete understanding of the information being presented for the purpose of encouraging a more thorough elaboration of the group member's feelings.

5. Encouragement—The skillful moderator should be aware of unresponsive members and try to break down their reserve and encourage their involvement.
6. Flexibility—While a predetermined outline of questions to be asked is beneficial, the moderator should be able to improvise and alter these plans amid the distractions of the group process.
7. Sensitivity—The moderator must be able to identify, as the group interview progresses, the informational level on which it is being conducted, and determine if it is appropriate for the subject under discussion.

Focus Group Constituency

The general consensus among marketing researchers seems to be that a focus group consists of eight to twelve members and a moderator. It is believed that fewer than eight group members places too great a burden on each member, whereas more than twelve tends to inhibit member participation.

With respect to group membership and selection, the focus group researcher should select participants from all relevant markets. For most businesses, relevant markets include such groups as past customers, present customers, as well as non-customers. The representation of multiple markets via group samples should allow the researcher to gain insight into potentially divergent viewpoints held by the different groups.

SUGGESTED FRAMEWORK

To this point, the discussion of focus group research has largely been from a conceptual and/or quasi-theoretical perspective. The following section sets forth an overall framework within which focus group research can be designed and conducted.

Step 1 requires the health care strategist to define the research question or problem in order to specify the objectives of the research as well as the initial direction of the group discussion. For example, the research question could center on methods to improve patient satisfaction, the feasibility of a new service or location, changes in operating policy, etc. The resulting question should ideally be broad enough to elicit an array of viewpoints from group members, yet pointed enough to prevent spurious conversation.

Step 2 requires the health care strategist to select the sample groupings. Ideally, the groupings should be proportionately comprised of all user markets. What percentage of one's patients are over 70? Under 25? Black? Male or Female? In each instance, a sample should be chosen so that its members are as similar as possible. Research suggests that the more socially and intellectually homogeneous the interview group, the more productive its reports. Otherwise, some comments made may be alien or meaningless to a majority of the group which in turn may cause them to withdraw from group interaction (Merton, Fiske and Kendall, 1956).

In many instances the research question(s) will determine group constituency. If you are interested in improving the level, quantity or type of patient services, then existing or past customers are obviously preferable. If market share maintenance is a selected topic, then past customers may offer much needed insight into this area.

How many focus group interviews should be conducted? Although there is no hard and fast rule, it stands to reason that at least one session should be held for each target market of importance to the organization. Where a particular segment is of prime importance, three or four sessions may be necessary. Furthermore, in the event the results of like groupings are in conflict, an additional session will be necessary to arrive at any meaningful conclusion(s).

Step 3 involves the selection of a group moderator. While the qualities sought in the group leader were discussed earlier, the sources of such a person have not been explored. Most of the published research on the subject suggests the retention of someone trained in the conduct of focus group research. Marketing research firms, consulting companies and university faculty are generally excellent sources for locating a focus group leader. In-house personnel have in the past been used with equivocal results. However, Feder (1983) suggests that it may be more beneficial to use those directly involved in the organization because of their knowledge of the subject matter.

A major contributor to the success of the project, in addition to proper training and experience, is perceived objectivity. If group members know the group leader or are aware of his/her affiliation with the sponsoring organization, then their willingness to "open-up" may be reduced significantly. It is critical that all group members perceive the moderator as being professional *and* objective.

Step 4 involves the actual conduct of the focus group interviews.

In addition to planning the topical area(s) to be covered, plans should be made to tape the sessions (video is preferable) for subsequent content analysis. The group sponsor may also find it informative to view the session by actually sitting-in during the interview or by observing through a one-way mirror. Such active or passive participation often allows the sponsor to glean additional meaning from the comments made as well as better associate responses with respondent characteristics. Based upon the outcome of a session, the sponsor and moderator may elect to redirect or modify some element(s) of future session in order to better meet the objectives/needs of the investigation.

Step 5 involves the analyzing and interpretation of the findings. After taping all interviews, the moderator alone or in combination with the practitioner will review all tapes and perform a content analysis in which the responses to all questions are evaluated and categorized. This classificatory procedure allows the moderator to draw qualified conclusions about user attitudes, perceptions, opinions, etc. regarding each area of inquiry.

It should be recognized that the preceding procedure is largely qualitative in nature. As such, subjectivity and the potential for bias introduction is a major obstacle to the successs of the process. For this reason, it is extremely important for the moderator to be skilled not only in the conduct of focus groups, but in the interpretation of its results as well.

Step 6 requires the health care strategist to translate these results in action plans. Based upon the data obtained, what changes, additions, deletions, etc. should be made in the health care product. Keown (1983) suggests that alternative actions can be classified into three groups. The "No-Action" group includes suggestions that are not feasible; for example, lack of parking space may be impossible to remedy due to the land/lease situation. The "Immediate Action" group requires minimum risk or financial involvement and has good face value; for example complaints about long waiting periods or unpleasant surroundings could easily be resolved by more efficient scheduling and housekeeping. "Further Research" represents an action grouping that would entail high risk and/or large financial outlays; for example, suggestions that a new and/or unusual medical service be offered. In such a case, the health care strategist may decide that additional quantitative research is required to determine the feasibility of that particular recommendation.

In most instances, it *is* necessary to validate or quantify focus group findings via a follow-up survey. For example, if focus group research indicates that patients are dissatisfied with office practice, billing procedures, lab hours, etc., then a self-reporting survey instrument should be designed and administered to an appropriate sample. If survey findings yield strong support for each of these "problem" areas, then the focus group results have been validated and appropriate responses can be devised.

CASE HISTORY

A large southeastern hospital had installed a corporate "wellness" program in early 1983. Approximately a year after its inception less than ten percent of all employees were participating in the program which had been installed at a substantial cost. After holding several conversations with hospital administrators, it was decided that focus group interviews would be conducted to explore the following:

1. The major reasons why employees were not participating in the corporate wellness program;
2. To identify any modification(s) that could be made in the program's content to increase participation, e.g., hours, location, programs, etc;
3. To explore user and nonuser perceptions of the program and its role, purpose, and objectives;
4. To identify educational objectives associated with the program, i.e., how could the hospital best communicate information about the program to its employees?

After determining the direction of the research (the preceding topics became the research objectives), the focus groups were formed. Selected from existing records were the names of eighty-four employees who were classified as either participants or non-participants in the "wellness" program. To the extent possible, groupings were established to achieve homogeneity (i.e., some groups consisted of nurses exclusively). Seven focus group interviews were ultimately conducted, two groups of participants and five groups of non-participants. Non-participant response was emphasized due to the significantly larger number of non-participative employees. Each group discussion was moderated, tape recorded, and content analyzed using the research criteria established at the onset of the project.

The moderator of the sessions was a graduate student in health care administration who had just completed study of "wellness" programs and focus group research. This person also simulated several interviews prior to the actual research process so as to gain focus group experience. Subsequent analysis was jointly performed by the moderator and the project's director, a faculty member at a nearby university.

The results obtained were then used as the basis for a follow-up survey of *all* hospital employees. Survey results supported many of the initial findings and conclusions drawn from the focus group interviews. For example, participants generally held a completely different attitude toward health and well-being when compared to non-participants. Those involved in the program displayed a greater responsibility for their own health compared to non-participants who relied heavily on medication or some form of passive health care. Further, participants wanted to see more varied types of programs (e.g., stress management, smoking cessation, diet planning, etc.) in addition to more "active" programs (e.g., jogging, basketball, racquetball, etc.).

Regarding the reasons for non-participation, the findings indicated that the types of programs offered as well as the time and location of such were the most prevalent reasons for their absence from the program. One of the more interesting findings obtained, which was originally identified in a focus group session, was non-participants' perceptions of why the hospital had established the program. A sizable number of non-participative employees felt that this was another "hospital ploy" to get more out of them. As such, many employees were not participating because of their misperceptions of the hospital's motivations.

In response to these findings, the hospital has since added a number of programs, increased the times and locations at which the programs are offered, arranged a baby sitting service, established all-male or all-female fitness groups, and issued a brochure outlining what the "wellness" program is, why it was established, what is available and cost (if any).

CONCLUSION

The case history previously cited illustrates the applicability of focus group research in providing useful qualitative information for a health care organization. In this instance, focus group research provided the foundation upon which a quantitative survey instrument was developed. This is not an isolated example. Focus group research is a tool gaining in popularity because of the unique insight it often provides. However, in most instances such qualitative research should not replace the more scientific approaches to marketing research. Focus group research can best be used as a complimentary tool to assist in problem definition as well as instrument and hypothesis development.

Focus group research is especially meaningful when the strategist is faced with a problem or issue with which he/she has little knowledge or direction. In such an instance, an initial response can often be formulated based upon the information obtained from the session. This information can then be converted into action plans or form the basis for further study.

REFERENCES

"Focus Group Interview: Consumers Rap About Today's Shopping, Buying," *Advertising Age*, (March 3, 1975), pp. 37-40.

Axelrod, Myril D. "10 Essentials for Good Qualitative Research," *Marketing News*, (February 28, 1975), pp. 6-7.

Bellenger, D. N., K. L. Bernhardt and J. L. Goldstucker (eds.). *Qualitative Research in Marketing*, (Chicago: American Marketing Association, 1976), pp. 7-28.

Chase, Donald A. "The Intensive Group Interview in Marketing," *MRA Viewpoints*, 1973.

Churchill, Gilbert A., Jr. *Marketing Research: Methodological Foundations*, (New York: Dryden Press, 1983), pp. 179-184.

Feder, R. A. "Media Research Report [focus group]," *Television/Radio Age*, 31 (December 5, 1983), p. 67.

Goldman, A. E. "The Group Depth Interview," *Journal of Marketing*, 26 (July 1962), pp. 61-68.

Hess, John M. "Group Interviewing," in G. S. Albaum and M. Venkatesan eds., *Scientific Marketing*, (Glencoe, IL: The Free Press, 1971), pp. 231-233.

Ingrassia, Lawrence, "A Matter of Taste: There's No Way to Tell if a New Food Product Will Please the Public," *The Wall Street Journal*, (February 26, 1980), pp. 1, 23.

Keown, Charles, "Focus Group Researach: Tool for the Retailer," *Journal of Small Business Management*, (April 1983), pp. 59-65.

Merton, R. K., M. Fiske and P. L. Kendall. *The Focused Interview*, (Glencoe, IL: The Free Press, 1956).

Munn, H. L. and W. L. Opdyke. "Group Interviews Reveal Consumer Buying Behavior," *Journal of Retailing*, (Fall, 1961), pp. 26-31.

Additional references the reader may wish to review on focus group research are the following:

ADDITIONAL REFERENCES

Adler, L. "To Learn What's on the Consumer's Mind, Try Some Focused Group Interviews," *Sales and Marketing Management*, 122 (April 9, 1979), pp. 76-77.

Cox, Keith K., J. B. Higginbotham and John Burton. "Applications of Focus Group Interviews in Marketing," *Journal of Marketing*, 40 (January 1976), pp. 77-80.

Egbert, Harry A. "Focus Groups: A Basic Tool to Probe Buyers' Attitudes," *Industrial Marketing*, 68 (March 1983), pp. 82-84.

Elrod, J. Mitchell, Jr. "Improving Employee Relations with Focus Groups," *Business*, 31 (November-December 1981), pp. 36-8.

Fern, Edward F. "The Use of Focus Groups for Idea Generation: The Effects of Group Size, Acquaintanceship, and Moderator on Response Quantity and Quality." *Journal of Marketing Research*, 19 (February 1982), pp. 1-13

Green, Michelle. "Test Marketing Hocus-Focus," *Madison Avenue*, 25 (November 1983), pp. 68, 71-73.

Holtzman, Eleanor. "Focus Group Moderators Should Be Well Versed in Interpretive Skills," *Marketing News*, 17 (February 18, 1983), p. 23.

Kover, Arthur J. "The Legitimacy of Qualitative Research," *Journal of Advertising Reserach*, 22 (December 1982), pp. 49-50.

Lubet, Margery J. "Focus Group Research: Planning is the Key," *Bank Marketing*, (December 1982), pp. 17-20.

Reynolds, Fred D. and D. K. Johnson. "Validity of Focus-Group Findings," *Journal of Advertising Research,* 18 (June 1970), pp. 21-24.

Szybillo, George J. and R. Berger. "What Advertising Agencies Think of Focus Groups," *Journal of Advertising Research*, 19 (June 1979), pp. 29-33.